NATIONAL ARCHIVES

MICROFILM RESOURCES FOR RESEARCH

A Comprehensive Catalog

NATIONAL ARCHIVES AND RECORDS ADMINISTRATION
WASHINGTON, DC

Foreword

The National Archives and Records Administration is responsible for administering and making available for research the permanently valuable noncurrent records of the federal government. These archival holdings, now amounting to more than 1.7 million cubic feet, date from the first days of the Continental Congress in 1774 and preserve the basic records of the legislative, judicial, and executive branches of government from that time to the present. The National Archives also administers the Presidential libraries.

These research resources document significant events in our nation's history, but most of them are preserved for their continuing practical use in ordinary processes of government. All nonrestricted records are available for the use of scholars, students, genealogists, and others.

Published for the
National Archives and Records Administration
by the National Archives Trust Fund Board
Revised 1996

Library of Congress Cataloging-in-Publication Data

United States.   National Archives and Records Administration.
    Microfilm resources for research : a comprehensive catalog /
National Archives.
        p.   cm.
    Includes index.
    ISBN 0-911333-34-7
    1. United States. National Archives and Records Administration—
Microfilm catalogs. 2. United States—History—Sources—
Bibliography—Microform catalogs. 3. Documents on microfilm—
United States—Catalogs. I. Title.
CD3026   1996
016.973—dc20

                                                        95-51100
                                                        CIP

Table of Contents

Introduction

The National Archives Microfilm Publications Program

Microfilm has been and continues to be an important way of distributing and preserving records. Since 1941 the National Archives has microfilmed federal records of high research interest to make the records available for researchers while preserving the original from deterioration and damage from handling. Copies of these microfilmed records are sold to the public, making these federal records accessible to libraries, research centers, and individuals.

The National Archives microfilm publications program provides ready access to records for research in a wide variety of fields, including history, economics, political science, law, and genealogy. This program emphasizes microfilming groups of records relating to the same general subject or to a specific geographic area. For example, many of the pension and compiled military service records and accompanying indexes for 19th-century volunteer soldiers are on microfilm. Microfilmed State Department records, such as consular despatches and notes, provide almost complete coverage of relations between the United States and other countries during the 19th and early 20th centuries.

This catalog, which lists more than 2,000 microfilm publications available from the National Archives, supersedes *National Archives Microfilm Resources for Research: A Comprehensive Catalog* (1990). The catalog is arranged by numbered record group, a system that groups records according to the agency that created them, generally at the bureau level. Donated materials and miscellaneous records are listed last.

Within each record group in this catalog, the microfilm publications are arranged to make them easy to use:

1. Similar records for various date spans, such as census records, are in chronological order:

> First Census of the United States,
> 1790.
> M637.   12 rolls.

> Second Census of the United States,
> 1800.
> M32.   52 rolls.

> Third Census of the United States.
> 1810.
> M252.   71 rolls.

2. Related records concerning foreign countries, such as despatches from U.S. ministers, are arranged alphabetically by country or city:

> Despatches From U.S. Ministers
> to Cuba, 1902–1906.
> T158.   18 rolls.

> Despatches From U.S. Ministers to the
> Dominican Republic, 1883–1906.
> M93.   15 rolls.

> Despatches From U.S. Ministers
> to Ecuador, 1848–1906.
> T50.   19 rolls.

3. Indexes and other users' tools generally precede the records they accompany. For example, the indexes to compiled service records of volunteer Union soldiers precede the compiled service records.

If no particular arrangement seems logical, the publications are listed in their own numerical order, with the M publication numbers preceding the A and T publication numbers.

Each entry gives the full title of the publication; the M, A, or T publication number; the number of rolls; and whether there is an accompanying descriptive pamphlet ("DP" signifying that a descriptive pamphlet exists). The film is on 35mm rolls unless the entry specifies 16mm or microfiche. Entries marked with a ➤ have been published since 1990. A typical entry appears as follows:

> ➤Records of the U.S. Morgan
> Horse Farm, 1907–1951.
> M1375. 12 rolls. DP.

The catalog does not include administrative histories, roll-by-roll lists, or descriptions of what is on the microfilm. Roll lists are available in DPs, in select catalogs, and from reference services at the Washington, DC, and College Park, MD, National Archives facilities and regional archives across the country.

This catalog includes a keyword index, an alphabetical list of record groups, and a numerical list of microfilm publication numbers. Both lists show the catalog page on which the record group begins or the microfilm publication appears.

Recent Accessions

The National Archives recently acquired approximately 40,000 rolls of microfilm from the biographic collections of the Berlin Documents Center. Some collections are still being processed at this printing, and the final number of rolls is undetermined. The documents consist of personnel and related records of the Nazi Party and affiliated organizations during the Third Reich. Finding aids to these records, including series descriptions and extant roll lists, are maintained in the Textual Research Room at Archives II. The microfilm is part of Record Group 242, National Archives Collection of Foreign Records Seized, 1941–. For general information on these collections, contact the Textual Reference Branch at 301-713-7250.

Types of Microfilm Publications

The National Archives reproduces records in two forms: microfilm rolls and microfiche. Rolls of film are wound on plastic reels, and each frame reproduces one or two single pages or items. A microfiche is a sheet of film containing multiple microimages in a grid pattern, and each microimage is a copy of one or two pages or items.

National Archives microfilm publications are divided into three types: M, A, and T publications. Most M publications reproduce an entire series of records. Usually, at the beginning of the first roll (sometimes on every roll) and on the first fiche, an introduction is reproduced that contains explanatory material to help researchers use the records. Each introduction consists of a general and brief history of the originating agency, a description of the records' content, and an explanation of the arrangement of the records. Some introductions also include special aids, such as indexes and appendixes. A table of contents of the microfilm publication follows the introduction. Many introductions and tables of contents are printed as accompanying descriptive pamphlets (DPs). DPs that are available (as shown in this catalog) may be requested by contacting the National Archives, Publications Distribution Branch (NECD), Room G9, Seventh and Pennsylvania Avenue, NW, Washington, DC 20408 (telephone 1-800-234-8861 or 202-501-7190; fax 202-501-7170).

A and T publications are numbered in the same sequence and, unlike M publications, do not always reproduce a complete series of records. They may contain only segments, by date or subject, of a larger series. In addition, A and T publications may be copies of microfilm produced by other federal agencies and accessioned by the National Archives. A and T publications are reproduced and sold exactly as they were filmed; they contain no introductions and have no accompanying descriptive pamphlets.

Index

The index lists proper names, place names, and key words from the publication titles in alphabetical order. These are followed by the M, A, or T numbers and page/column numbers (e.g., "17.3" means page 17, column 3).

Consular posts are listed only under appropriate country and state names. Entries for censuses under state names refer only to the Soundex publications, not to the actual census schedules.

How to Get More Information

For more information on specific publications and roll lists, please contact the National Archives, Publications Distribution Branch (NECD), Room G9, Seventh and Pennsylvania Avenue, NW, Washington, DC 20408 (telephone 1-800-234-8861 or 202-501-7190; fax 202-501-7170).

Other Catalogs of Microfilm Publications

Individual microfilm publications are described in more detail in a series of catalogs of select microfilm publications. These catalogs, which relate to subjects of high research interest, provide roll-by-roll lists and contain detailed descriptions of the records. The catalogs in the series are:

- 1790 –1890 Federal Population Censuses (1995)
- 1900 Federal Population Census (1996)
- 1910 Federal Population Census (1996)
- Immigrant & Passenger Arrivals (1991)
- Military Service Records (1985)
- Black Studies (1996)
- American Indians (1995)
- Genealogical & Biographical Research (1983)
- Diplomatic Records (1986)
- Federal Court Records (1987)

For information about fees and the ordering of catalogs, please contact the National Archives, Publications Distribution Branch (NECD), Room G9, Seventh and Pennsylvania Avenue, NW, Washington, DC 20408 (telephone 1-800-234-8861 or 202-501-7190; fax 202-501-7170).

How to Order Microfilm

All microfilm publications of National Archives records are for sale. You can buy either individual rolls or fiche or a complete set (all rolls or fiche). The prices as of May 15, 1996, are $34 a roll and $4.25 a fiche for positive film copies (U.S. orders), but these prices are subject to change without advance notice. The prices for foreign orders are $39 a roll and $4.65 a fiche. Shipping is included in these prices. The minimum order is $6 for fiche.

A check or money order made payable to the "National Achives Trust Fund (NECD)" must accompany each order. Orders may also be charged to *VISA* or *MasterCard* accounts. Government agencies, educational institutions, and businesses may purchase microfilm on an accounts-receivable basis but must submit purchase orders. Mail orders to the National Archives Trust Fund (NECD), P.O. Box 100793, Atlanta, GA 30384-0793.

When ordering microfilm, please state the microfilm publication number; if you are not buying a complete set, also state the specific roll or fiche number(s) you wish to purchase.

If you need more information on how to order, details of specific shipping charges, or help identifying which rolls of a publication you wish to purchase, please contact the National Archives, Publications Distribution Branch (NECD), Room G9, Seventh and Pennsylvania Avenue, NW, Washington, DC 20408 (telephone 1-800-234-8861 or 202-501-7190; fax 202-501-7170).

Copies of National Archives microfilm publications may also be purchased from Scholarly Resources, Inc., 104 Greenhill Avenue, Wilmington, DE 19805 (telephone 302-654-7713; fax 302-654-3871; e-mail sales@scholarly.com). Copies available for sale from other sources have not been authorized or duplicated by the National Archives and may be one or more generations removed from the master materials—adversely affecting the quality and legibility of each image.

Microfilm Specifications

All microfilm sold through the National Archives microfilm publications program is silver-halide positive microfilm. Rolls are 35mm or 16mm reel microfilm on plastic reels. Reduction ratios range from 12.1 to 20.1; the number of frames on each reel varies. Microfiche are cards measuring 105mm by 148.75mm (approximately 4 by 6 inches). Reduction ratios range from 24:1 to 32:1; the number of images on each fiche varies.

In some instances, it is possible to obtain microfilm in a different form (e.g., duplicate negative rather than positive). If you desire such services, please contact the National Archives, Publications Distribution Branch (NECD), Room G9, Seventh and Pennsylvania Avenue, NW, Washington, DC 20408 (telephone 1-800-234-8861 or 202-501-7190; fax 202-501-7170).

Microfilm Publications Arranged by Record Group Number

Records of the Bureau of Entomology and Plant Quarantine. RG 7

Letters Received by the Bureau of Entomology From W. D. Hunter, May 5, 1902–Nov. 23, 1908.
M864.   3 rolls.   DP.

Records of the National Recovery Administration. RG 9

Document Series of the National Recovery Administration, 1933–1936.
M213.   186 rolls.   DP.   16mm.

National Recovery Administration's *Blue Eagle*, a Weekly Newspaper, June 11, 1934–May 17, 1935.
T692.   1 roll.

General Records of the United States Government. RG 11

Enrolled Original Acts and Resolutions of the U.S. Congress, 1789–1823.
M337.   17 rolls.

Certificates of Ratification of the Constitution and the Bill of Rights, Including Related Correspondence and Rejections of Proposed Amendments, 1787–1792.
M338.   1 roll.

Ratified Indian Treaties, 1722–1869.
M668.   16 rolls.   DP.

Executive Orders, 1–7521, 1862–1936.
M1118.   17 rolls.   DP.

Perfected International Treaties ("Treaty Series"), 1778–1945.
M1247.   56 rolls available.

Enrolled Acts and Resolutions of Congress, 1893–1956.
M1326.   139 rolls.

Numerical List of Presidential Proclamations, 1–2317, 1789–1938.
M1331.   1 roll.

➤Ratified Amendments XI–XXVI to the United States Constitution.
M1518.   16 rolls.   DP.

Index to Presidential Proclamations, 1789–1947.
T279.   2 rolls.

Presidential Proclamations, 1–2160, 1789–1936.
T1223.   11 rolls.

Records of the Office of Education. RG 12

Letters Sent by the Commissioner of Education, 1870–1909.
M635.   71 rolls.   DP.

Records of the Veterans Administration. RG 15

Schedules Enumerating Union Veterans and Widows of Union Veterans of the Civil War, 1890.
M123.   118 rolls.

Index to War of 1812 Pension Application Files.
M313.   102 rolls.   DP.

Revolutionary War Pension and Bounty-Land Warrant Application Files.
M804.   2,670 rolls.   DP.

Selected Records From Revolutionary War Pension and Bounty-Land Warrant Application Files.
M805.   898 rolls.   DP.

Veterans Administration Pension Payment Cards, 1907–1933.
M850.   2,539 rolls.   DP.

Virginia Half Pay and Other Related Revolutionary War Pension Application Files.
M910.   18 rolls.   DP.

Case Files of Disapproved Pension Applications of Widows and Other Dependents of Civil War and Later Navy Veterans ("Navy Widows' Originals"), 1861–1910.
M1274.   Approx. 8,500   DP. cards (microfiche).

Case Files of Approved Pension Applications of Widows and Other Dependents of Civil War and Later Navy Veterans ("Navy Widows' Certificates"), 1861–1910.
M1279.   Approx. 40,000   DP. cards (microfiche).

Lists of Navy Veterans for Whom There are Navy Widows' and Other Dependents' Disapproved Pension Files ("Navy Widows' Originals"), 1861–1910.
M1391.   15 cards (microfiche).   DP.

➤Index to Pension Application Files of Remarried Widows Based on Service in the War of 1812, Indian Wars, Mexican War, and Regular Army Before 1861.
M1784.   1 roll.

➤Index to Pension Application Files of Remarried Widows Based on Service in the Civil War and Later Wars and in the Regular Army After the Civil War.
M1785.   7 rolls.

➤Record of Invalid Pension Payments to Veterans of the Revolutionary War and the Regular Army and Navy, March 1801–September 1815.
M1786.   1 roll.

General Index to Pension Files,
1861–1934.
T288.   544 rolls.   16mm.

Organization Index to Pension Files of
Veterans Who Served Between 1861
and 1900.
T289.   765 rolls.   16mm.

Old War Index to Pension Files,
1815–1926.
T316.   7 rolls.   16mm.

Index to Mexican War Pension Files,
1887–1926.
T317.   14 rolls.   16mm.

Index to Indian War Pension Files,
1892–1926.
T318.   12 rolls.   16mm.

Selected Pension Application Files
Relating to the Mormon Battalion,
Mexican War, 1846–1848.
T1196.   21 rolls.

Records of the Office of the Secretary of Agriculture. RG 16

Letters Sent by the Assistant
Secretary of Agriculture, 1889–1894.
M122.   16 rolls.

Letters Sent by the Secretary of
Agriculture, 1893–1929.
M440.   563 rolls.   DP.

Records of the Bureau of Animal Industry. RG 17

➤Records of the U.S. Morgan Horse
Farm, 1907–1951.
M1375.   12 rolls.   DP.

Records of the Army Air Forces. RG 18

Mission and Combat Reports of the
Fifth Fighter Command, 1942–1945.
M1065.   9 rolls.   DP.

Missing Air Crew Reports of the U.S.
Army Air Forces, 1942–1947.
M1380.   5,990 cards (microfiche).

Records of the Bureau of Ships. RG 19

Index to the General Photographs of
the Bureau of Ships, 1914–1946.
M1157.   9 rolls.   16mm.

Captured Japanese Ships' Plans and
Design Data.
M1176.   10 rolls.

General Photographs of the Bureau of
Ships, 1914.
M1222.   1,100 rolls.

Records of District Courts of the United States. RG 21

Indexes to the Naturalization Records
of the U.S. District Court for the District
and Territory of Alaska, 1900–1929.
M1241.   1 roll.   DP.

Naturalization Records of the U.S.
District Courts for the State of Alaska,
1900–1924.
M1539.   5 rolls.

➤Naturalization Records of the U.S.
District Court for the Territory of
Arizona, 1864–1915.
M1615.   5 rolls.

➤Naturalization Records of the U.S.
District Court for the District of
Arizona, 1912–1955.
M1616.   7 rolls.

Admiralty Case Files of the U.S.
District Court for the Northern District
of California, 1850–1900.
M1249.   401 rolls.   DP.

➤Naturalization Index Cards of the
United States District Court for the
Southern District of California, Central
Division, Los Angeles, 1915–1976.
M1525.   14 rolls.   DP.

➤Index Cards to Overseas Military
Petitions of the U.S. District Court for
the Southern District of California,
Central Division (Los Angeles),
1943–1945, 1954, 1955–1956.
M1606.   2 rolls.

➤Index Cards to Civil Case Files of
the U.S. District Court for the Southern
District of California, Southern Division
(San Diego), January 1955 to June
1962.
M1735.   1 roll.

➤Index Cards to Criminal Case Files
of the U.S. District Court for the
Southern District of California,
Southern Division (San Diego),
January 1955 to June 1962.
M1736.   2 rolls.

➤Index Cards to Civil and Criminal Case
Files of the U.S. District Court for the
Southern District of California,
Southern Division (San Diego),
July 1962 to August 1966.
M1737.   3 rolls.

➤Index to Naturalization Records of
the U.S. District Court for the Southern
District of California, Central Division,
Los Angeles, 1887–1937.
M1607.   2 rolls.

➤Index Cards to Bankruptcy, Civil, and
Criminal Case Files of the U.S. District
Court for the Southern District of
California, Southern Division
(San Diego), 1953 to 1954.
M1741.   1 roll.

➤Naturalization Records of the United
States District Court for the Southern
District of California, Central Division,
Los Angeles, 1887–1940.
M1524.   244 rolls.   DP.

Records of the U.S. District Court for
the Northern District of California and
Predecessor Courts, 1851–1950.
T717.   125 rolls.

Private Land Grant Cases in the Circuit
Court of the Northern District of
California, 1852–1910.
T1207.   28 rolls.

Index to Private Land Grant Cases,
U.S. District Court, Northern District of
California, 1853–1903.
T1214.   1 roll.

Index to Private Land Grant Cases,
U.S. District Court, Southern District of
California.
T1215.   1 roll.

Index by County to Private Land Grant
Cases, U.S. District Court, Northern
and Southern Districts of California.
T1216.   1 roll.

Selected Indexes to Naturalization
Records of the U.S. Circuit and District
Courts, Northern District of California,
1852–1928.
T1220.   3 rolls.

Naturalization Records Created by the U.S.
District Courts in Colorado, 1877–1952.
M1192.   79 rolls.

➤Records of the U.S. District and Circuit
Courts for the District of Connecticut:
Documents Relating to the Various Cases
Involving the Spanish Schooner Amistad.
M1753.   1 roll.

➤Index to Naturalization Petitions for the U.S. Circuit Court, 1795–1911, and District Court, 1795–1928, for the District of Delaware.
M1649.   1 roll.

➤Naturalization Petitions of the U.S. District and Circuit Courts for the District of Delaware, 1795–1930.
M1644.   19 rolls.

Records of the U.S. District Court for the District of Columbia Relating to Slaves, 1851–1863.
M433.   3 rolls.

Habeas Corpus Case Records, 1820–1863, of the U.S. Circuit Court for the District of Columbia.
M434.   2 rolls.

Minutes of the U.S. Circuit Court for the District of Columbia, 1801–1863.
M1021.   6 rolls.   DP.

Admiralty Final Record Books of the U.S. District Court for the Southern District of Florida (Key West), 1828–1911.
M1360.   19 rolls.   DP.

Index Books, 1789–1928, and Minutes and Bench Dockets, 1789–1870, for the U.S. District Court, Southern District of Georgia.
M1172.   3 rolls.   DP.

Minutes of the U.S. Circuit Court for the District of Georgia, 1790–1842, and Index to Plaintiffs and Defendants in the Circuit Courts, 1790–1860.
M1184.   3 rolls.   DP.

➤Lincoln at the Bar: Selected Case Files from the United States District and Circuit Courts, Southern District of Illinois, 1855–1861.
M1530.   7 rolls.   DP.

Records of the U.S. District Court for the Eastern District of Louisiana, 1806–1814.
M1082.   18 rolls.   DP.

Land Claim Case Files of the U.S. District Court for the Eastern District of Louisiana, 1844–1880.
M1115.   16 rolls.

Minutes of the U.S. Circuit Court for the District of Maryland, 1790–1911.
M931.   7 rolls.   DP.

Criminal Case Files of the U.S. Circuit Court for the District of Maryland, 1795–1860.
M1010.   4 rolls.   DP.

Act of 1800 Bankruptcy Case Files of the U.S. District Court for the District of Maryland, 1800–1803.
M1031.   2 rolls.   DP.

Indexes to Naturalization Petitions to the U.S. Circuit and District Courts for Maryland, 1797–1951.
M1168.   25 rolls.   DP.

➤Naturalization Petitions of the U.S. District Court for the District of Maryland, 1906–1930.
M1640.   43 rolls.

➤Index to Naturalization Petitions and Records of the U.S. District Court, 1906–1966, and the U.S. Circuit Court, 1906–1911, for the District of Massachusetts.
M1545.   115 rolls.

Petitions and Records of Naturalization of the U.S. District Court and Circuit Courts of the District of Massachusetts, 1906–1929.
M1368.   330 rolls.

Records of the Territorial Court of Michigan, 1815–1836.
M1111.   9 rolls.   DP.

Indexes to Naturalization Records of the Montana Territorial and Federal Courts, 1868–1929.
M1236.   1 roll.   DP.

Naturalization Records of the U.S. District Courts for the State of Montana, 1891–1929.
M1538.   3 rolls.

Records of the U.S. District Court for the District of New Jersey and Predecessor Courts, 1790–1950.
T928.   186 rolls.   16mm.

Minutes, Trial Notes, and Rolls of Attorneys of the U.S. Circuit Court for the Southern District of New York, 1790–1841.
M854.   3 rolls.   DP.

Appellate Case Files of the U.S. Circuit Court for the Southern District of New York, 1793–1845.
M855.   8 rolls.   DP.

Judgment Records of the U.S. Circuit Court for the Southern District of New York, 1794–1840.
M882.   8 rolls.   DP.

Law Case Files of the U.S. Circuit Court for the Southern District of New York, 1790–1846.
M883.   43 rolls.   DP.

Equity Case Files of the U.S. Circuit Court for the Southern District of New York, 1791–1846.
M884.   23 rolls.   DP.

Criminal Case Files of the U.S. Circuit Court for the Southern District of New York, 1790–1853.
M885.   6 rolls.   DP.

Minutes and Rolls of Attorneys of the U.S. District Court for the Southern District of New York, 1789–1841.
M886.   9 rolls.   DP.

Admiralty Case Files of the U.S. District Court for the Southern District of New York, 1790–1842.
M919.   62 rolls.   DP.

Prize and Related Records for the War of 1812 of the U.S. District Court for the Southern District of New York, 1812–1816.
M928.   9 rolls.   DP.

Act of 1800 Bankruptcy Records of the U.S. District Court for the Southern District of New York, 1800–1809.
M933.   11 rolls.   DP.

Judgment Records of the U.S. District Court for the Southern District of New York, 1795–1840.
M934.   16 rolls.   DP.

Law Case Files of the U.S. District Court for the Southern District of New York, 1795–1844.
M937.   15 rolls.   DP.

Records of the Clerk of the Court, 1746–1932, and of the U.S. Commissioners, 1837–1860, of the U.S. District Court for the Southern District of New York.
M938.   1 roll.   DP.

Case Papers of the Court of Admiralty of the State of New York, 1784–1788.
M948.   1 roll.   DP.

Case Files in Suits Involving Consuls and Vice Consuls and the Repeal of Patents of the U.S. District Court for the Southern District of New York, 1806–1860.
M965.   2 rolls.   DP.

➤Index to Naturalization Petitions of the United States District Court for the Eastern District of New York, 1865–1957.
M1164.   142 rolls.   DP.

➤Index (Soundex) to Naturalization Petitions Filed in Federal, State, and Local Courts in New York, New York, Including New York, Kings, Queens, and Richmond Counties, 1792–1906.
M1674.   294 rolls.

➤Alphabetical Index to Declarations of Intention of the U.S. District Court for the Southern District of New York, 1917–50.
M1675.   111 rolls.

➤Alphabetical Index to Petitions for Naturalization of the U.S. District Court for the Southern District of New York, 1824–1941.
M1676.   102 rolls.

➤Alphabetical Index to Petitions for Naturalization of the U.S. District Court for the Western District of New York, 1906–1966.
M1677.   20 rolls.

Records of the Vice Admiralty Court of the Province of New York.
T842.   1 roll.

Confederate Papers of the U.S. District Court for the Eastern District of North Carolina, 1861–1865.
M436.   1 roll.

Minute Books, U.S. District Court, Eastern District of North Carolina, Albemarle Division at Edenton, 1807–70, and at Elizabeth City, 1870–1914.
M1425.   1 roll.   DP.

Minute Books, U.S. District Court, Eastern District of North Carolina, Cape Fear Division at Wilmington, 1795–96
and 1858–1911.
M1426.   2 rolls.   DP.

Minute Books, U.S. District Court, Eastern District of North Carolina, Pamlico Division at New Bern, 1858–1914.
M1427.   2 rolls.

Minute Books, U.S. Circuit Court, Eastern District of North Carolina, Raleigh, 1791–1866.
M1428.   2 rolls.   DP.

Admiralty Final Record Books, U.S. District Court, Eastern District of North Carolina, 1858–1907.
M1429.   1 roll.   DP.

Confederate Court Records, Eastern District of North Carolina, 1861–1864.
M1430.   1 roll.   DP.

Index to the Naturalization Records of the U.S. District Court for Oregon, 1859–1956.
M1242.   3 rolls.   DP.

➤Naturalization Records of the U.S. District Court for the District of Oregon, 1859–1941.
M1540.   62 rolls.

Minutes of the U.S. Circuit Court for the Eastern District of Pennsylvania, 1790–1844.
M932.   2 rolls.   DP.

War of 1812 Prize Case Files of the U.S. District Court for the Eastern District of Pennsylvania, 1812–1815.
M966.   2 rolls.   DP.

Law and Appellate Records of the U.S. Circuit Court for the Eastern District of Pennsylvania, 1790–1847.
M969.   26 rolls.   DP.

Equity Records of the U.S. Circuit Court for the Eastern District of Pennsylvania, 1790–1847.
M985.   23 rolls.   DP.

Criminal Case Files of the U.S. Circuit Court for the Eastern District of Pennsylvania, 1791–1840.
M986.   7 rolls.   DP.

Records of the U.S. Circuit Court for the Western District of Pennsylvania, 1801–1802, and Minutes and Habeas Corpus and Criminal Case Files of the U.S. District Court for the Eastern District of Pennsylvania, 1789–1843.
M987.   3 rolls.   DP.

Admiralty Case Files of the U.S. District Court for the Eastern District of Pennsylvania, 1789–1840.
M988.   18 rolls.   DP.

Information Case Files, 1789–1843, and Related Records, 1792–1918, of the U.S. District Court for the Eastern District of Pennsylvania.
M992.   10 rolls.   DP.

Act of 1800 Bankruptcy Records of the U.S. District Court for the Eastern District of Pennsylvania, 1800–1806.
M993.   24 rolls.   DP.

Law (Civil Action) Records for the U.S. District Court for the Eastern District of Pennsylvania, 1789–1844.
M1057.   40 rolls.   DP.

Indexes to Registers and Registers of Declarations of Intention and Petitions for Naturalization of the U.S. District and Circuit Courts for the Western District of Pennsylvania, 1820–1906.
M1208.   3 rolls.   DP.

Indexes to Naturalization Petitions to the U.S. Circuit and District Courts for the Eastern District of Pennsylvania, 1795–1951.
M1248.   60 rolls.   DP.

➤Naturalization Petitions of the U.S. Circuit and District Courts for the Middle District of Pennsylvania, 1906–1930.
M1626.   123 rolls.

➤Naturalization Petitions for the Eastern District of Pennsylvania.
M1522.   369 rolls.

➤Naturalization Petitions of the U.S. District Court, 1820–1930, and Circuit Court, 1820–1911, for the Western District of Pennsylvania.
M1537.   437 rolls.

➤Landing Reports of Aliens from the U.S. District Court for the Eastern District of Pennsylvania, 1798–1828.
M1639.   1 roll.

Records of the U.S. District Court for the Eastern District of Pennsylvania Containing Statements of Fact in Forfeiture Cases, 1792–1918.
T819.   1 roll.

Pre-Federal Admiralty Court Records, Province and State of South Carolina, 1716–1789.
M1180.   3 rolls.   DP.

Minutes, Circuit and District Courts, District of South Carolina, 1789–1849, and Index to Judgments, Circuit and District Courts, 1792–1874.
M1181.   2 rolls.   DP.

Admiralty Final Record Books and Minutes for the U.S. District Court, District of South Carolina, 1790–1857.
M1182.   4 rolls.   DP.

Record of Admissions to Citizenship, District of South Carolina, 1790–1906.
M1183.   1 roll.   DP.

Final Record Books of the U.S. Circuit Court for West Tennessee, 1808–1839, and of the U.S. Circuit Court for the Middle District of Tennessee, 1839–1865.
M1212.   10 rolls.   DP.

Minute Books of the U.S. District Court for West Tennessee, 1797–1839, and of the U.S. District Court for the Middle District of Tennessee, 1839–1865.
M1213.   1 roll.   DP.

Minute Books of the U.S. Circuit Court for West Tennessee, 1808–1839, and of the U.S. Circuit Court for the Middle District of Tennessee, 1839–1864.
M1214.   4 rolls.   DP.

Final Record Books of the U.S. District Court for West Tennessee, 1803–1839, and of the U.S. District Court for the Middle District of Tennessee, 1839–1850; Land Claims Records for West Tennessee, 1807–1820.
M1215.   1 roll.   DP.

►Index to Naturalization Records of the U.S. District Court for the Eastern District of Tennessee at Chattanooga, 1888–1955.
M1611.   1 roll.

►Equity Case Files from the Western District Court of Texas at El Paso Relating to the Chinese Exclusion Acts, 1892–1915.
M1610.   34 rolls.   DP.

Territorial Case Files of the U.S. District Courts of Utah, 1870–1896.
M1401.   38 rolls.   DP.

Admiralty Case Files of the U.S. District Court for the Eastern District of Virginia, 1801–1861.
M1300.   18 rolls.   DP.

Case Papers of the U.S. District Court for the Eastern District of Virginia, 1863–1865, Relating to the Confiscation of Property.
M435.   1 roll.

►Naturalization Petitions of the U.S. District Court for the Western District of Virginia (Abingdon), 1914–1929.
M1645.   2 rolls.

►Naturalization Petitions of the U.S. District Court for the Western District of Virginia (Charlottesville), 1910–1929.
M1646.   1 roll.

►Naturalization Petitions of the U.S. District Court for the Eastern District of Virginia (Richmond), 1906–1929.
M1647.   10 rolls.

►Naturalization Petitions of the U.S. District Court for the Eastern District of Virginia (Alexandria), 1909–1920.
M1648.   5 rolls.

Indexes to Naturalization Records of the U.S. District Court for Western Washington, Northern Division (Seattle), 1890–1952.
M1232.   6 rolls   DP.

Indexes to Naturalization Records of the King County Territorial and Superior Courts, 1864–1889 and 1906–1928.
M1233.   1 roll.   DP.

Indexes to Naturalization Records of the Thurston County Territorial and Superior Courts, 1850–1974.
M1234.   2 rolls.   DP.

Indexes to Naturalization Records of the Snohomish County Territorial and Superior Courts, 1876–1974.
M1235.   3 rolls.   DP.

Indexes to Naturalization Records of the U.S. District Court, Western District of Washington, Southern Division (Tacoma), 1890–1953.
M1237.   2 rolls.   DP.

Indexes to Naturalization Records of the Pierce County Territorial and Superior Courts, 1853–1923.
M1238.   2 rolls.   DP.

►Naturalization Records of the U.S. District Court for the Eastern District of Washington, 1890–1972.
M1541.   40 rolls.

►Naturalization Records of the U.S. District Court for the Western District of Washington, 1890–1957.
M1542.   153 rolls.

►Naturalization Records of the Superior Courts for King, Pierce, Thurston, and Snohomish Counties, Washington, 1850–1974.
M1543.   103 rolls.

►U.S. District Court of Washington Rolls of Attorneys, 1890–1959.
M1618.   1 roll.

►Naturalization Petitions of the U.S. District Court for the Northern District of West Virginia, Wheeling, 1856–1867.
M1643.   2 rolls.

Naturalization Records of U.S. District Courts in the Southeast, 1790–1958.
M1547.   107 rolls.

Trial of Aaron Burr and Harman Blennerhassett, 1808.
T265.   1 roll.

Records of the U.S. Civil Commission at Memphis, 1863–1864.
T410.   9 rolls.

Records of the U.S. Fish and Wildlife Service. RG 22

"Alaska File" of the Office of the Secretary of the Treasury, 1868–1903.
M720.   25 rolls.   DP.

Records of the Coast and Geodetic Survey. RG 23

Correspondence of A. D. Bache, Superintendent of the Coast and Geodetic Survey, 1843–1865.
M642.   281 rolls.   DP.

Selected Tide-Staff Readings and Hydrographic Survey Soundings of Rear Adm. Robert E. Peary, USN, 1908–1909 North Polar Expedition.
T296.   1 roll.

Records of the Bureau of Naval Personnel. RG 24

Abstracts of Service Records of Naval Officers ("Records of Officers"), 1798–1893.
M330.   19 rolls.

Logbooks and Journals of the U.S.S. *Constitution*, 1798–1934.
M1030.   16 rolls.   DP.8.

Abstracts of Service Records of Naval Officers ("Records of Officers"), 1829–1924.
M1328.   18 rolls.   DP.

Logbooks of PT 109 (President Kennedy).
T576.   1 roll.

Index to Rendezvous Reports, Before and After the Civil War, 1846–1861, 1865–1884.
T1098.   32 rolls.   16mm.

Index to Rendezvous Reports, Civil War, 1861–1865.
T1099.   31 rolls.   16mm.

Index to Rendezvous Reports, Naval Auxiliary Service, 1917–1918.
T1100.   1 roll.   16mm.

Index to Rendezvous Reports, Armed Guard Personnel, 1917–1920.
T1101.   3 rolls.   16mm.

Index to Officers' Jackets, 1913–1925 ("Officers Directory").
T1102.   2 rolls.

Records of the U.S. Coast Guard. RG 26

Lighthouse Letters, 1792–1809.
M63.   3 rolls.

Lighthouse Deeds and Contracts, 1790–1853.
M94.   2 rolls.

Alaska File of the Revenue Cutter Service, 1867–1914.
M641.   20 rolls.   DP.

Registers of Lighthouse Keepers, 1845–1912.
M1373.   6 rolls.

U.S. Coast Guard Reports of Assistance to Individuals and Vessels, 1916–1940.
T720.   247 rolls.

Index by District to U.S. Coast Guard Reports of Assistance, 1917–1938.
T919.   19 rolls.   16mm.

Index by Station to U.S. Coast Guard Reports of Assistance, 1924–1938.
T920.   9 rolls.   16mm.

Index by Floating Unit to U.S. Coast Guard Reports of Assistance, 1917–1935.
T921.   5 rolls.   16mm.

U.S. Coast Guard Casualty and Wreck Reports, 1913–1939.
T925.   21 rolls.   16mm.

Index to U.S. Coast Guard Casualty and Wreck Reports, 1913–1939.
T926.   7 rolls.   16mm.

Records of the Weather Bureau. RG 27

The Maury Abstract Logs, 1796–1861.
M1160.   88 rolls.   DP.

Selected Records From Records of the Weather Bureau Relating to New Orleans, 1841–1907.
M1379.   8 rolls.   DP.

Journal of the Lockwood Expedition on the North Coast of Greenland, Apr. 31–June 1, 1882.
T298.   1 roll.

Climatological Records of the Weather Bureau, 1819–1892.
T907.   564 rolls.

Records of the Post Office Department. RG 28

Letters Sent by the Postmaster General, 1789–1836.
M601.   50 rolls.   DP.

Record of Appointment of Postmasters, Oct. 1789–1832.
M1131.   4 rolls.

Record of Appointment of Postmasters, 1832–Sept. 30, 1971.
M841.   145 rolls.   DP.

Post Office Department Reports of Site Locations, 1837–1950.
M1126.   683 rolls.   DP.

Journal of Hugh Finlay, Surveyor of Post Roads and Post Offices, 1773–1774; and Accounts of the General Post Office in Philadelphia and of the Various Deputy Postmasters— "The Ledger of Benjamin Franklin"— Jan. 1775–Jan. 1780.
T268.   1 roll.

Records of the Bureau of the Census. RG 29
Federal Population Decennial Census Schedules

First Census of the United States, 1790.
M637.   12 rolls.

Second Census of the United States, 1800.
M32.   52 rolls.

Third Census of the United States, 1810.
M252.   71 rolls.

Fourth Census of the United States, 1820.
M33.   142 rolls.

Fifth Census of the United States, 1830.
M19.   201 rolls.

Sixth Census of the United States, 1840.
M704.   580 rolls.

Seventh Census of the United States, 1850.
M432.   1,009 rolls.

Eighth Census of the United States, 1860.
M653.   1,438 rolls.

Ninth Census of the United States, 1870.
M593.   1,748 rolls.

Minnesota Census Schedules for 1870.
T132.   13 rolls.

Tenth Population Census

Tenth Census of the United States, 1880.
T9.   1,454 rolls.

Index (Soundex) to the 1880 Population Schedules for Alabama.
T734.   74 rolls.   16mm.

Index (Soundex) to the 1880 Population Schedules for Arizona.
T735.   2 rolls.   16mm.

Index (Soundex) to the 1880 Population Schedules for Arkansas.
T736.   48 rolls.   16mm.

Index (Soundex) to the 1880 Population Schedules for California.
T737.   34 rolls.   16mm.

Index (Soundex) to the 1880 Population Schedules for Colorado.
T738.   7 rolls.   16mm.

Index (Soundex) to the 1880 Population Schedules for Connecticut.
T739.   25 rolls.   16mm.

Index (Soundex) to the 1880 Population Schedules for Dakota Territory.
T740.   6 rolls.   16mm.

Index (Soundex) to the 1880 Population Schedules for Delaware.
T741.   9 rolls.   16mm.

Index (Soundex) to the 1880 Population Schedules for the District of Columbia.
T742.   9 rolls.   16mm.

Index (Soundex) to the 1880 Population Schedules for Florida.
T743.   16 rolls.   16mm.

Index (Soundex) to the 1880 Population Schedules for Georgia.
T744.   86 rolls.   16mm.

Index (Soundex) to the 1880 Population Schedules for Idaho Territory.
T745.   2 rolls.   16mm.

Index (Soundex) to the 1880 Population Schedules for Illinois.
T746.   143 rolls.   16mm.

Index (Soundex) to the 1880 Population Schedules for Indiana.
T747.   98 rolls.   16mm.

Index (Soundex) to the 1880 Population Schedules for Iowa.
T748.   78 rolls.   16mm.

Index (Soundex) to the 1880 Population Schedules for Kansas.
T749.   51 rolls.   16mm.

Index (Soundex) to the 1880 Population Schedules for Kentucky.
T750.   83 rolls.   16mm.

Index (Soundex) to the 1880 Population Schedules for Louisiana.
T751.   55 rolls.   16mm.

Index (Soundex) to the 1880 Population Schedules for Maine.
T752.   29 rolls.   16mm.

Index (Soundex) to the 1880 Population Schedules for Maryland.
T753.   47 rolls.   16mm.

Index (Soundex) to the 1880 Population Schedules for Massachusetts.
T754.   70 rolls.   16mm.

Index (Soundex) to the 1880 Population Schedules for Michigan.
T755.   73 rolls.   16mm.

Index (Soundex) to the 1880 Population Schedules for Minnesota.
T756.   37 rolls.   16mm.

Index (Soundex) to the 1880 Population Schedules for Mississippi.
T757.   69 rolls.   16mm.

Index (Soundex) to the 1880 Population Schedules for Missouri.
T758.   114 rolls.   16mm.

Index (Soundex) to the 1880 Population Schedules for Montana Territory.
T759.   2 rolls.   16mm.

Index (Soundex) to the 1880 Population Schedules for Nebraska.
T760.   22 rolls.   16mm.

Index (Soundex) to the 1880 Population Schedules for Nevada.
T761.   3 rolls.   16mm.

Index (Soundex) to the 1880 Population Schedules for New Hampshire.
T762.   13 rolls.   16mm.

Index (Soundex) to the 1880 Population Schedules for New Jersey.
T763.   49 rolls.   16mm.

Index (Soundex) to the 1880 Population Schedules for New Mexico Territory.
T764.   6 rolls.   16mm.

Index (Soundex) to the 1880 Population Schedules for New York.
T765.   187 rolls.   16mm.

Index (Soundex) to the 1880 Population Schedules for North Carolina.
T766.   79 rolls.   16mm.

Index (Soundex) to the 1880 Population Schedules for Ohio.
T767.   143 rolls.   16mm.

Index (Soundex) to the 1880 Population Schedules for Oregon.
T768.   8 rolls.   16mm.

Index (Soundex) to the 1880 Federal Schedules for Pennsylvania.
T769.   168 rolls.   16mm.

Index (Soundex) to the 1880 Population Schedules for Rhode Island.
T770.   11 rolls.   16mm.

Index (Soundex) to the 1880 Population Schedules for South Carolina.
T771.   56 rolls.   16mm.

Index (Soundex) to the 1880 Population Schedules for Tennessee.
T772.   86 rolls.   16mm.

Index (Soundex) to the 1880 Population Schedules for Texas.
T773.   77 rolls.   16mm.

Index (Soundex) to the 1880 Population Schedules for Utah Territory.
T774.   7 rolls.   16mm.

Index (Soundex) to the 1880 Population Schedules for Vermont.
T775.   15 rolls.   16mm.

Index (Soundex) to the 1880 Population Schedules for Virginia.
T776.   82 rolls.   16mm.

Index (Soundex) to the 1880 Population Schedules for Washington Territory.
T777.   4 rolls.   16mm.

Index (Soundex) to the 1880 Population Schedules for West Virginia.
T778.   32 rolls.   16mm.

Index (Soundex) to the 1880 Population Schedules for Wisconsin.
T779.   51 rolls.   16mm.

Index (Soundex) to the 1880 Population Schedules for Wyoming.
T780.   1 roll.   16mm.

Eleventh Population Census

Eleventh Census of the United States, 1890.
M407.   3 rolls.

Index to the Eleventh Census of the United States, 1890.
M496.   2 rolls.   16mm.

Twelfth Population Census

Twelfth Census of the United States, 1900.
T623.   1,854 rolls.

Index (Soundex) to the 1900 Federal Population Census Schedules for Alabama.
T1030.   177 rolls.   16mm.

Index (Soundex) to the 1900 Federal Population Census Schedules for Alaska.
T1031.   15 rolls.   16mm.

Index (Soundex) to the 1900 Federal Population Census Schedules for Arizona.
T1032.   22 rolls.   16mm.

Index (Soundex) to the 1900 Federal Population Census Schedules for Arkansas.
T1033.   135 rolls.   16mm.

Index (Soundex) to the 1900 Federal Population Census Schedules for California.
T1034.   198 rolls.   16mm.

Index (Soundex) to the 1900 Federal Population Census Schedules for Colorado.
T1035.   69 rolls.   16mm.

Index (Soundex) to the 1900 Federal Population Census Schedules for Connecticut.
T1036.   107 rolls.   16mm.

Index (Soundex) to the 1900 Federal Population Census Schedules for Delaware.
T1037.   21 rolls.   16mm.

Index (Soundex) to the 1900 Federal Population Census Schedules for the District of Columbia.
T1038.   42 rolls.   16mm.

Index (Soundex) to the 1900 Federal Population Census Schedules for Florida.
T1039.   62 rolls.   16mm.

Index (Soundex) to the 1900 Federal Population Census Schedules for Georgia.
T1040.   214 rolls.   16mm.

Index (Soundex) to the 1900 Federal Population Census Schedules for Hawaii.
T1041.   30 rolls.   16mm.

Index (Soundex) to the 1900 Federal Population Census Schedules for Idaho.
T1042.   19 rolls.   16mm.

Index (Soundex) to the 1900 Federal Population Census Schedules for Illinois.
T1043.   475 rolls.   16mm.

Index (Soundex) to the 1900 Federal Population Census Schedules for Indiana.
T1044.   254 rolls.   16mm.

Index (Soundex) to the 1900 Federal Population Census Schedules for Iowa.
T1045.   212 rolls.   16mm.

Index (Soundex) to the 1900 Federal Population Census Schedules for Kansas.
T1046.   148 rolls.   16mm.

Index (Soundex) to the 1900 Federal Population Census Schedules for Kentucky.
T1047.   1200 rolls.   16mm.

Index (Soundex) to the 1900 Federal Population Census Schedules for Louisiana.
T1048.   146 rolls.   16mm.

Index (Soundex) to the 1900 Federal Population Census Schedules for Maine.
T1049.   80 rolls.   16mm.

Index (Soundex) to the 1900 Federal Population Census Schedules for Maryland.
T1050.   127 rolls.   16mm.

Index (Soundex) to the 1900 Federal Population Census Schedules for Massachusetts.
T1051.   319 rolls.   16mm.

Index (Soundex) to the 1900 Federal Population Census Schedules for Michigan.
T1052.   257 rolls.   16mm.

Index (Soundex) to the 1900 Federal Population Census Schedules for Minnesota.
T1053.   180 rolls.   16mm.

Index (Soundex) to the 1900 Federal Population Census Schedules for Mississippi.
T1054.   156 rolls.   16mm.

Index (Soundex) to the 1900 Federal Population Census Schedules for Missouri.
T1055.   300 rolls.   16mm.

Index (Soundex) to the 1900 Federal Population Census Schedules for Montana.
T1056.   40 rolls.   16mm.

Index (Soundex) to the 1900 Federal Population Census Schedules for Nebraska.
T1057.   107 rolls.   16mm.

Index (Soundex) to the 1900 Federal Population Census Schedules for Nevada.
T1058.   7 rolls.   16mm.

Index (Soundex) to the 1900 Federal Population Census Schedules for New Hampshire.
T1059.   52 rolls.   16mm.

Index (Soundex) to the 1900 Federal Population Census Schedules for New Jersey.
T1060.   204 rolls.   16mm.

Index (Soundex) to the 1900 Federal Population Census Schedules for New Mexico.
T1061.   23 rolls.   16mm.

Index (Soundex) to the 1900 Federal Population Census Schedules for New York.
T1062.   768 rolls.   16mm.

Index (Soundex) to the 1900 Federal Population Census Schedules for North Carolina.
T1063.   168 rolls.   16mm.

Index (Soundex) to the 1900 Federal Population Census Schedules for North Dakota.
T1064.   36 rolls.   16mm.

Index (Soundex) to the 1900 Federal Population Census Schedules for Ohio.
T1065.   397 rolls.   16mm.

Index (Soundex) to the 1900 Federal Population Census Schedules for Oklahoma.
T1066.   42 rolls.   16mm.

Index (Soundex) to the 1900 Federal Population Census Schedules for Oregon.
T1067.   54 rolls.   16mm.

Index (Soundex) to the 1900 Federal Population Census Schedules for Pennsylvania.
T1068.   611 rolls.   16mm.

Index (Soundex) to the 1900 Federal Population Census Schedules for Rhode Island.
T1069.   49 rolls.   16mm.

Index (Soundex) to the 1900 Federal Population Census Schedules for South Carolina.
T1070.   124 rolls.   16mm.

Index (Soundex) to the 1900 Federal Population Census Schedules for South Dakota.
T1071.   44 rolls.   16mm.

Index (Soundex) to the 1900 Federal Population Census Schedules for Tennessee.
T1072.   188 rolls.   16mm.

Index (Soundex) to the 1900 Federal Population Census Schedules for Texas.
T1073.   286 rolls.   16mm.

Index (Soundex) to the 1900 Federal Population Census Schedules for Utah.
T1074.   29 rolls.   16mm.

Index (Soundex) to the 1900 Federal Population Census Schedules for Vermont.
T1075.   41 rolls.   16mm.

Index (Soundex) to the 1900 Federal Population Census Schedules for Virginia.
T1076.   174 rolls.   16mm.

Index (Soundex) to the 1900 Federal Population Census Schedules for Washington.
T1077.   69 rolls.   16mm.

Index (Soundex) to the 1900 Federal Population Census Schedules for West Virginia.
T1078.   93 rolls.   16mm.

Index (Soundex) to the 1900 Federal Population Census Schedules for Wisconsin.
T1079.   189 rolls.   16mm.

Index (Soundex) to the 1900 Federal Population Census Schedules for Wyoming.
T1080.   15 rolls.   16mm.

Index (Soundex) to the 1900 Federal Population Census Schedules for Military and Naval.
T1081.   32 rolls.   16mm.

Index (Soundex) to the 1900 Federal Population Census Schedules for Indian Territory.
T1082.   42 rolls.   16mm.

Index (Soundex) to the 1900 Federal Population Census Schedules for Institutions.
T1083.   8 rolls.   16mm.

Thirteenth Population Census

Thirteenth Census of the United States, 1910.
T624.   1,784 rolls.

Index (Soundex) to the 1910 Federal Population Census Schedules for Alabama.
T1259.   140 rolls.   16mm.

Index (Miracode) to the 1910 Federal Population Census Schedules for Arkansas.
T1260.   139 rolls.   16mm.

Index (Miracode) to the 1910 Federal Population Census Schedules for California.
T1261.   272 rolls.   16mm.

Index (Miracode) to the 1910 Federal Population Census Schedules for Florida.
T1262.   84 rolls.   16mm.

Index (Soundex) to the 1910 Federal Population Census Schedules for Georgia.
T1263.   174 rolls.   16mm.

Index (Miracode) to the 1910 Federal Population Census Schedules for Illinois.
T1264.   491 rolls.   16mm.

Index (Miracode) to the 1910 Federal Population Census Schedules for Kansas.
T1265.   145 rolls.   16mm.

Index (Miracode) to the 1910 Federal Population Census Schedules for Kentucky.
T1266.   194 rolls.   16mm.

Index (Miracode and Soundex) to the 1910 Federal Population Census Schedules for Louisiana.
T1267.   132 rolls.   16mm.

Index (Miracode) to the 1910 Federal Population Census Schedules for Michigan.
T1268.   253 rolls.   16mm.

Index (Soundex) to the 1910 Federal Population Census Schedules for Mississippi.
T1269.   118 rolls.   16mm.

Index (Miracode) to the 1910 Federal Population Census Schedules for Missouri.
T1270.   285 rolls.   16mm.

Index (Miracode) to the 1910 Federal Population Census Schedules for North Carolina.
T1271.   178 rolls.   16mm.

Index (Miracode) to the 1910 Federal Population Census Schedules for Ohio.
T1272.   418 rolls.   16mm.

Index (Miracode) to the 1910 Federal Population Census Schedules for Oklahoma.
T1273.   143 rolls.   16mm.

Index (Miracode) to the 1910 Federal Population Census Schedules for Pennsylvania.
T1274.   688 rolls.   16mm.

Index (Soundex) to the 1910 Federal Population Census Schedules for South Carolina.
T1275.   93 rolls.   16mm.

Index (Soundex) to the 1910 Federal Population Census Schedules for Tennessee.
T1276.   142 rolls.   16mm.

Index (Soundex) to the 1910 Federal Population Census Schedules for Texas.
T1277.   262 rolls.   16mm.

Index (Miracode) to the 1910 Federal Population Census Schedules for Virginia.
T1273.   183 rolls.   16mm.

Index (Miracode) to the 1910 Federal Population Census Schedules for West Virginia.
T1279.   108 rolls.   16mm.

Fourteenth Population Census

➤Fourteenth Census of the United States, 1920.
T625.   2,076 rolls.

➤Index (Soundex) to the 1920 Federal Population Census Schedules for Alabama.
M1548.   159 rolls.   16mm.

➤Index (Soundex) to the 1920 Federal Population Census Schedules for Arizona.
M1549.   30 rolls.   16mm.

➤Index (Soundex) to the 1920 Federal Population Census Schedules for Arkansas.
M1550.   131 rolls.   16mm.

➤Index (Soundex) to the 1920 Federal Population Census Schedules for California.
M1551.   327 rolls.   16mm.

➤Index (Soundex) to the 1920 Federal Population Census Schedules for Colorado.
M1552.   80 rolls.   16mm.

➤Index (Soundex) to the 1920 Federal Population Census Schedules for Connecticut.
M1553.   111 rolls.   16mm.

➤Index (Soundex) to the 1920 Federal Population Census Schedules for Delaware.
M1554.   20 rolls.   16mm.

➤Index (Soundex) to the 1920 Federal Population Census Schedules for District of Columbia.
M1555.   49 rolls.   16mm.

➤Index (Soundex) to the 1920 Federal Population Census Schedules for Florida.
M1556.   74 rolls.   16mm.

➤Index (Soundex) to the 1920 Federal Population Census Schedules for Georgia.
M1557.   200 rolls.   16mm.

➤Index (Soundex) to the 1920 Federal Population Census Schedules for Idaho.
M1558. 33 rolls. 16mm.

➤Index (Soundex) to the 1920 Federal Population Census Schedules for Illinois.
M1559. 510 rolls. 16mm.

➤Index (Soundex) to the 1920 Federal Population Census Schedules for Indiana.
M1560. 230 rolls. 16mm.

➤Index (Soundex) to the 1920 Federal Population Census Schedules for Iowa.
M1561. 181 rolls. 16mm.

➤Index (Soundex) to the 1920 Federal Population Census Schedules for Kansas.
M1562. 129 rolls. 16mm.

➤Index (Soundex) to the 1920 Federal Population Census Schedules for Kentucky.
M1563. 180 rolls. 16mm.

➤Index (Soundex) to the 1920 Federal Population Census Schedules for Louisiana.
M1564. 135 rolls. 16mm.

➤Index (Soundex) to the 1920 Federal Population Census Schedules for Maine.
M1565. 67 rolls. 16mm.

➤Index (Soundex) to the 1920 Federal Population Census Schedules for Maryland.
M1566. 126 rolls. 16mm.

➤Index (Soundex) to the 1920 Federal Population Census Schedules for Massachusetts.
M1567. 326 rolls. 16mm.

➤Index (Soundex) to the 1920 Federal Population Census Schedules for Michigan.
M1568. 291 rolls. 16mm.

➤Index (Soundex) to the 1920 Federal Population Census Schedules for Minnesota.
M1569. 174 rolls. 16mm.

➤Index (Soundex) to the 1920 Federal Population Census Schedules for Mississippi.
M1570. 123 rolls. 16mm.

➤Index (Soundex) to the 1920 Federal Population Census Schedules for Missouri.
M1571. 269 rolls. 16mm.

➤Index (Soundex) to the 1920 Federal Population Census Schedules for Montana.
M1572. 46 rolls. 16mm.

➤Index (Soundex) to the 1920 Federal Population Census Schedules for Nebraska.
M1573. 96 rolls. 16mm.

➤Index (Soundex) to the 1920 Federal Population Census Schedules for Nevada.
M1574. 9 rolls. 16mm.

➤Index (Soundex) to the 1920 Federal Population Census Schedules for New Hampshire.
M1575. 40 rolls. 16mm.

➤Index (Soundex) to the 1920 Federal Population Census Schedules for New Jersey.
M1576. 253 rolls. 16mm.

➤Index (Soundex) to the 1920 Federal Population Census Schedules for New Mexico.
M1577. 31 rolls. 16mm.

➤Index (Soundex) to the 1920 Federal Population Census Schedules for New York.
M1578. 885 rolls. 16mm.

➤Index (Soundex) to the 1920 Federal Population Census Schedules for North Carolina.
M1579. 166 rolls. 16mm.

➤Index (Soundex) to the 1920 Federal Population Census Schedules for North Dakota.
M1580. 48 rolls. 16mm.

➤Index (Soundex) to the 1920 Federal Population Census Schedules for Ohio.
M1581. 476 rolls. 16mm.

➤Index (Soundex) to the 1920 Federal Population Census Schedules for Oklahoma.
M1582. 155 rolls. 16mm.

➤Index (Soundex) to the 1920 Federal Population Census Schedules for Oregon.
M1583. 69 rolls. 16mm.

➤Index (Soundex) to the 1920 Federal Population Census Schedules for Pennsylvania.
M1584. 712 rolls. 16mm.

➤Index (Soundex) to the 1920 Federal Population Census Schedules for Rhode Island.
M1585. 53 rolls. 16mm.

➤Index (Soundex) to the 1920 Federal Population Census Schedules for South Carolina.
M1586. 112 rolls. 16mm.

➤Index (Soundex) to the 1920 Federal Population Census Schedules for South Dakota.
M1587. 48 rolls. 16mm.

➤Index (Soundex) to the 1920 Federal Population Census Schedules for Tennessee.
M1588. 162 rolls. 16mm.

➤Index (Soundex) to the 1920 Federal Population Census Schedules for Texas.
M1589. 373 rolls. 16mm.

➤Index (Soundex) to the 1920 Federal Population Census Schedules for Utah.
M1590. 33 rolls. 16mm.

➤Index (Soundex) to the 1920 Federal Population Census Schedules for Vermont.
M1591. 32 rolls. 16mm.

➤Index (Soundex) to the 1920 Federal Population Census Schedules for Virginia.
M1592. 168 rolls. 16mm.

➤Index (Soundex) to the 1920 Federal Population Census Schedules for Washington.
M1593. 118 rolls. 16mm.

➤Index (Soundex) to the 1920 Federal Population Census Schedules for West Virginia.
M1594. 109 rolls. 16mm.

➤Index (Soundex) to the 1920 Federal Population Census Schedules for Wisconsin.
M1595. 196 rolls. 16mm.

➤Index (Soundex) to the 1920 Federal Population Census Schedules for Wyoming.
M1596. 17 rolls. 16mm.

➤Index (Soundex) to the 1920 Federal Population Census Schedules for Alaska.
M1597. 6 rolls. 16mm.

➤Index (Soundex) to the 1920 Federal Population Census Schedules for Hawaii.
M1598.   24 rolls.   16mm.

➤Index (Soundex) to the 1920 Federal Population Census Schedules for the Panama Canal Zone.
M1599.   3 rolls.   16mm.

➤Index (Soundex) to the 1920 Federal Population Census Schedules for Military-Naval Districts.
M1600.   18 rolls.   16mm.

➤Index (Soundex) to the 1920 Federal Population Census Schedules for Puerto Rico.
M1601.   33 rolls.   16mm.

➤Index (Soundex) to the 1920 Federal Population Census Schedules for Guam.
M1602.   1 roll.   16mm.

➤Index (Soundex) to the 1920 Federal Population Census Schedules for American Samoa.
M1603.   2 rolls.   16mm.

➤Index (Soundex) to the 1920 Federal Population Census Schedules for the Virgin Islands.
M1604.   3 rolls.   16mm.

➤Index (Soundex) to the 1920 Federal Population Census Schedules for Institutions.
M1605.   1 roll.   16mm.

Federal Nonpopulation Census Schedules

➤Nonpopulation Census Schedules for the District of Columbia, 1850–1870: Agriculture, Industry, Mortality, and Social Statistics, and Nonpopulation Census Schedules for Worcester County, Maryland, 1850: Agriculture.
M1793.   1 roll.

Nonpopulation Census Schedules for Georgia, 1850–1880.
T1137.   27 rolls.

Nonpopulation Census Schedules for Illinois, 1850–1880.
T1133.   64 rolls.

Nonpopulation Census Schedules for Iowa, 1850–1880.
T1156.   62 rolls.

Nonpopulation Census Schedules for Kansas, 1850–1880.
T1130.   48 rolls.

➤Nonpopulation Census Schedules for Kentucky, 1850–1880.
M1528.   42 rolls.

Nonpopulation Census Schedules for Louisiana, 1850–1880.
T1136.   15 rolls.

➤Nonpopulation Census Schedules for Baltimore City and County, Maryland, 1850–1860: Agriculture, Industry, and Social Statistics.
M1799.   1 roll.

Nonpopulation Census Schedules for Massachusetts, 1850–1880.
T1204.   40 rolls.

Nonpopulation Census Schedules for Michigan, 1850–1880 (in the custody of the Michigan State Archives).
T1164.   77 rolls.

Nonpopulation Census Schedules for Michigan, 1850: Mortality Schedules (in the custody of the State Library of Ohio).
T1163.   1 roll.

➤Nonpopulation Census Schedules for Minnesota, 1860: Agriculture.
M1802.   1 roll.

Nonpopulation Census Schedules for Nebraska, 1860–1880.
T1128.   16 rolls.

➤Manufacturing Schedules Contained in the 1810 Population Census Schedules of New York State.
M1792.   1 roll.

Nonpopulation Census Schedules for Ohio, 1850–1880.
T1159.   104 rolls.

Nonpopulation Census Schedules for Pennsylvania, 1850–1860: Manufactures Schedules.
T1157.   9 rolls.

Nonpopulation Census Schedules for Pennsylvania, 1850–1880: Social Statistics and Supplemental Schedules.
M597.   23 rolls.

Nonpopulation Census for Pennsylvania, 1850–1880: Agriculture.
T1138.   62 rolls.

➤Nonpopulation Census Schedules for Pennsylvania, 1870–1880: Industry and Manufacturing.
M1796.   9 rolls.

Nonpopulation Census Schedules for Tennessee, 1850–1880.
T1135.   39 rolls.

Nonpopulation Census Schedules for Texas, 1850–1880.
T1134.   59 rolls.

➤Nonpopulation Census Schedules for Vermont, 1850–1870: Agriculture and Industry.
M1798.   9 rolls.

➤Nonpopulation Census Schedules for Utah Territory and Vermont, 1870: Mortality.
M1807.   1 roll.

Nonpopulation Census Schedules for Virginia, 1850–1880.
T1132.   34 rolls.

Nonpopulation Census Schedules for Washington Territory, 1860–1880.
A1154.   8 rolls.

Federal Mortality Census Schedules, 1850–1880 (formerly in the custody of the Daughters of the American Revolution), and Related Indexes.
T655.   30 rolls.

Records of the 1820 Census of Manufactures.
M279.   27 rolls.   DP.

State and Special Census Schedules

Schedules of the Minnesota Territory Census of 1857.
T1175.   5 rolls.

Schedules of the Colorado State Census of 1885.
M158.   8 rolls.   DP.

Schedules of the Florida State Census of 1885.
M845.   13 rolls.   DP.

Schedules of the Nebraska State Census of 1885.
M352.   56 rolls.   DP.

Schedules of the New Mexico Territory Census of 1885.
M846.   6 rolls.   DP.

➤Schedules of a Special Census of Indians, 1880
M1791.   5 rolls.   DP.

➤Third Census of the United States, 1810. Population Schedules, Washington County, Ohio.
M1803.   1 roll.

➤Eighth Census of the United States for the Northern District of Halifax County, Virginia, 1860: Schedules of Free Inhabitants, Slave Inhabitants, Mortality, Agriculture, Industry, and Social Statistics.
M1808. 1 roll.

➤First Territorial Census for Oklahoma, 1890.
M1811. 1 roll.

Other Census Records
Cross Index to Selected City Street and Enumeration Districts, 1910 Census.
M1283. 50 cards (microfiche).

Publications of the Bureau of the Census: 1790 Census, Printed Schedules.
T498. 3 rolls.

Publications of the Bureau of the Census, 1790–1916.
T825. 42 rolls.

Descriptions of Census Enumeration Districts, 1900.
T1210. 10 rolls.

Descriptions of Census Enumeration Districts, 1830–1890 and 1910–1950.
T1224. 146 rolls.

Records of the Extension Service. RG 33
Photographs of the Federal Extension Service, 1920–1954 (S Series).
M1146. 13 rolls.

Photographs of the Federal Extension Service, 1920–1945 (SC Series).
M1147. 11 rolls.

Extension Service Annual Reports: Alabama, 1909–1944.
T845. 115 rolls. 16mm.

Extension Service Annual Reports: Alaska, 1930–1944.
T846. 2 rolls. 16mm.

Extension Service Annual Reports: Arizona, 1915–1944.
T847. 22 rolls. 16mm.

Extension Service Annual Reports: Arkansas, 1909–1944.
T848. 106 rolls. 16mm.

Extension Service Annual Reports: California, 1913–1944.
T849. 54 rolls. 16mm.

Extension Service Annual Reports: Colorado, 1913–1944.
T850. 77 rolls. 16mm.

Extension Service Annual Reports: Connecticut, 1913–1944.
T851. 30 rolls. 16mm.

Extension Service Annual Reports: Delaware, 1914–1944.
T852. 13 rolls. 16mm.

Extension Service Annual Reports: District of Columbia, 1917–1919.
T853. 1 roll. 16mm.

Extension Service Annual Reports: Florida, 1909–1944.
T854. 46 rolls. 16mm.

Extension Service Annual Reports: Georgia, 1909–1944.
T855. 141 rolls. 16mm.

Extension Service Annual Reports: Hawaii, 1929–1944.
T856. 7 rolls. 16mm.

Extension Service Annual Reports: Idaho, 1913–1944.
T857. 47 rolls. 16mm.

Extension Service Annual Reports: Illinois, 1914–1944.
T858. 82 rolls. 16mm.

Extension Service Annual Reports: Indiana, 1912–1944.
T859. 80 rolls. 16mm.

Extension Service Annual Reports: Iowa, 1912–1944.
T860. 195 rolls. 16mm.

Extension Service Annual Reports: Kansas, 1913–1944.
T861. 186 rolls. 16mm.

Extension Service Annual Reports: Kentucky, 1912–1944.
T862. 89 rolls. 16mm.

Extension Service Annual Reports: Louisiana, 1909–1944.
T863. 67 rolls. 16mm.

Extension Service Annual Reports: Maine, 1915–1944.
T864. 48 rolls. 16mm.

Extension Service Annual Reports: Maryland, 1912–1944.
T865. 70 rolls. 16mm.

Extension Service Annual Reports: Massachusetts, 1914–1944.
T866. 59 rolls. 16mm.

Extension Service Annual Reports: Michigan, 1913–1944.
T867. 77 rolls. 16mm.

Extension Service Annual Reports: Minnesota, 1914–1944.
T868. 105 rolls. 16mm.

Extension Service Annual Reports: Mississippi, 1909–1944.
T869. 96 rolls. 16mm.

Extension Service Annual Reports: Missouri, 1914–1944.
T870. 90 rolls. 16mm.

Extension Service Annual Reports: Montana, 1914–1944.
T871. 64 rolls. 16mm.

Extension Service Annual Reports: Nebraska, 1913–1944.
T872. 89 rolls. 16mm.

Extension Service Annual Reports: Nevada, 1915–1944.
T873. 19 rolls. 16mm.

Extension Service Annual Reports: New Hampshire, 1914–1944.
T874. 37 rolls. 16mm.

Extension Service Annual Reports: New Jersey, 1913–1944.
T875. 45 rolls. 16mm.

Extension Service Annual Reports: New Mexico, 1914–1944.
T876. 30 rolls. 16mm.

Extension Service Annual Reports: New York, 1912–1944.
T877. 90 rolls. 16mm.

Extension Service Annual Reports: North Carolina, 1909–1944.
T878. 144 rolls. 16mm.

Extension Service Annual Reports: North Dakota, 1912–1944.
T879. 68 rolls. 16mm.

Extension Service Annual Reports: Ohio, 1915–1944.
T880. 98 rolls. 16mm.

Extension Service Annual Reports: Oklahoma, 1909–1944.
T881. 135 rolls. 16mm.

Extension Service Annual Reports: Oregon, 1914–1944.
T882. 73 rolls. 16mm.

Extension Service Annual Reports: Pennsylvania, 1914–1944.
T883. 43 rolls. 16mm.

Extension Service Annual Reports: Puerto Rico, 1930–1944.
T884. 14 rolls. 16mm.

Extension Service Annual Reports:
Rhode Island, 1914–1944.
T885.   12 rolls.   16mm.

Extension Service Annual Reports:
South, 1913–1914.
T886.   1 roll.   16mm.

Extension Service Annual Reports:
South Carolina, 1909–1944.
T887.   91 rolls.   16mm.

Extension Service Annual Reports:
South Dakota, 1913–1944.
T888.   65 rolls.   16mm.

Extension Service Annual Reports:
Tennessee, 1910–1944.
T889.   64 rolls.   16mm.

Extension Service Annual Reports:
Texas, 1909–1944.
T890.   182 rolls.   16mm.

Extension Service Annual Reports:
Utah, 1914–1944.
T891.   30 rolls.   16mm.

Extension Service Annual Reports:
Vermont, 1912–1944.
T892.   31 rolls.   16mm.

Extension Service Annual Reports:
Virginia, 1908–1944.
T893.   82 rolls.   16mm.

Extension Service Annual Reports:
Washington, 1913–1944.
T894.   45 rolls.   16mm.

Extension Service Annual Reports:
West Virginia, 1912–1944.
T895.   47 rolls.   16mm.

Extension Service Annual Reports:
Wisconsin, 1913–1944.
T896.   49 rolls.   16mm.

Extension Service Annual Reports:
Wyoming, 1914–1944.
T897.   37 rolls.   16mm.

Records of the Civilian Conservation Corps. RG 35

➤Civilian Conservation Corps
Newspaper, "Happy Days,"
1933–1940.
M1783.   6 rolls.

Records of the U.S. Customs Service. RG 36

See also Records of the Immigration
and Naturalization Service, RG 85.

Passenger Lists, Vessel Lists, and Indexes

Indexes to Passenger and Vessel Lists

Index to Passenger Lists of Vessels
Arriving at Baltimore, Maryland,
1833–1866.
M326.   22 rolls.   DP.   16mm.

Index to Passenger Lists of Vessels
Arriving at Baltimore, Maryland,
1820–1897 (Federal Passenger Lists).
M327.   171 rolls.   DP.   16mm.

Index to Passenger Lists of Vessels
Arriving at Boston, Massachusetts,
1848–1891.
M265.   282 rolls.   DP.   16mm.

Index to Passenger Lists of Vessels
Arriving at New Orleans, Louisiana,
1853–1899.
T527.   32 rolls.   16mm.

Index to Passenger Lists of Vessels
Arriving at New York, New York,
1820–1846.
M261.   103 rolls.   DP.   16mm.

Index to Passenger Lists of Vessels
Arriving at Philadelphia, Pennsylvania,
1800–1906.
M360.   151 rolls.   DP.   16mm.

Supplemental Index to Passenger
Lists of Vessels Arriving at Atlantic and
Gulf Coast Ports (Excluding New
York), 1820–1874.
M334.   188 rolls.   DP.   16mm.

Passenger Lists

Passenger Lists of Vessels Arriving
at Baltimore, Maryland, 1820–1891.
M255.   50 rolls.   DP.

Quarterly Abstracts of Passenger Lists
of Vessels Arriving at Baltimore,
Maryland, 1820–1869.
M596.   6 rolls.   DP.

Passenger Lists of Vessels Arriving at
Boston, Massachusetts, 1820–1891.
M277.   115 rolls.   DP.

Passenger Lists of Vessels Arriving at
New Orleans, Louisiana, 1820–1902.
M259.   93 rolls.   DP.

Quarterly Abstracts of Passenger Lists
of Vessels Arriving at New Orleans,
Louisiana, 1820–1875.
M272.   17 rolls.   DP.

Passenger Lists of Vessels Arriving at
New York, New York, 1820–1897.
M237.   675 rolls.   DP.

Passenger Lists of Vessels Arriving at
Philadelphia, Pennsylvania, 1800–
1882.
M425.   108 rolls.   DP.

Copies of Lists of Passengers Arriving
at Miscellaneous Ports on the Atlantic
and Gulf Coasts and at Ports on the
Great Lakes, 1820–1873.
M575.   16 rolls.   DP.

Vessel Lists

Registers of Vessels Arriving at the Port
of New York, New York, From Foreign
Ports, 1789–1919.
M1066.   27 rolls.   DP.

Other Records

Letters and Reports Received by the
Secretary of the Treasury From Special
Agents, 1854–1861.
M177.   3 rolls.   DP.

Alaska File of the Special Agents
Division of the Department of the
Treasury, 1867–1903.
M802.   16 rolls.   DP.

Records of Alaskan Custom Houses,
1867–1939.
T1189.   131 rolls.

Computer-Processed Tabulations of
Data From Seamen's Protective
Certificate Applications to the Collector
of Customs for the Port of Philadelphia,
1812–1815.
M972.   1 roll.   DP.

Records of the Collector of Customs for
the Collection District of New London,
Connecticut, 1789–1938.
M1162.   57 rolls.

➤U.S. Customs, Puget Sound District
Log Books and Shipping Articles, ca.
1890–1937.
M1633.   68 rolls.

Impost Books of the Collector of
Customs at Philadelphia, 1789–1804.
T255.   6 rolls.

Records of the Hydrographic Office. RG 37

Records of the U.S. Exploring Expedition Under the Command of Lt. Charles Wilkes, 1836–1842.
M75.   27 rolls.   DP.

Records of the Office of the Chief of Naval Operations. RG 38

Selected Naval Attache Reports Relating to the World Crisis, 1937–1943.
M975.   3 rolls.   DP.

Subject Index to Naval Intelligence Reports, 1940–1946.
M1332.   20 rolls.   DP.

➤U.S. Submarine War Patrol Reports, 1941–1945.
M1752.   1,155 cards DP.
             (microfiche).

General Records of the Department of Commerce. RG 40

General Correspondence of the Office of the Secretary of Commerce, 1929–1933.
M838.   16 rolls.   DP.

Minutes of the Industrial Commission, 1898–1902.
T10.   1 roll.

Records of the Bureau of Marine Inspection and Navigation. RG 41

Certificates of Registry, Enrollment, and License Issued at Edgartown, Massachusetts, 1815–1913.
M130.   9 rolls.   DP.

Vessel Documentation Records From the Port of Pembina, North Dakota, 1885–1959.
M1339.   10 rolls.

Vessel Licenses and Enrollments From the Port of St. Louis, Missouri, 1835–1944.
M1340.   26 rolls.

➤Merchant Marine License Applications, Puget Sound District, 1888–1910.
M1632.   3 rolls.

Records of the Office of Public Buildings and Public Parks of the National Capital. RG 42

Records of the District of Columbia Commissioners and of the Offices Concerned With Public Buildings, 1791–1867.
M371.   27 rolls.   DP.

Records of International Conferences, Commissions, and Expositions. RG 43

Records of the Department of State Relating to the First Panama Congress, 1825–1827.
M662.   1 roll.   DP.

Records of the Department of State Relating to the Paris Peace Commission, 1898.
T954.   3 rolls.

Records of the American Delegation, U.S.-USSR Joint Commission on Korea, and Records Relating to the United Nations Temporary Commission on Korea (UNTCOK), 1945–1948.
M1243.   23 rolls.   DP.

Records of the Office of Government Reports. RG 44

Minutes of the Executive Council, July 11, 1933–Nov. 13, 1934.
T37.   1 roll.

Proceedings of the National Emergency Council, Dec. 19, 1933–April 28, 1936.
T38.   1 roll.

Naval Records Collection of the Office of Naval Records and Library. RG 45

Records of the Office of the Secretary of the Navy

Letters Received by the Secretary of the Navy From Commanding Officers of Squadrons ("Squadron Letters"), 1841–1886.
M89.   300 rolls.   DP.

Miscellaneous Letters Received by the Secretary of the Navy 1801–1884.
M124.   647 rolls.   DP.

Letters Received by the Secretary of the Navy From Captains ("Captains' Letters"), 1805–1861, 1866–1885.
M125.   413 rolls.   DP.

Letters Received by the Secretary of the Navy From Commanders, 1804–1886.
M147.   124 rolls.   DP.

Letters Received by the Secretary of the Navy From Commissioned Officers Below the Rank of Commander and From Warrant Officers ("Officers' Letters"), 1802–1884.
M148.   518 rolls.   DP.

Letters Received by the Secretary of the Navy From the President and Executive Agencies, 1837–1886.
M517.   49 rolls.   DP.   16mm.

Letters Received by the Secretary of the Navy From Chiefs of Navy Bureaus, 1842–1885.
M518.   33 rolls.   DP.   16mm.

Letters Received by the Secretary of the Navy From Navy Agents and Naval Storekeepers, 1843–1865.
M528.   12 rolls.   DP.

Letters Received by the Secretary of the Navy From the Attorney General of the United States Containing Legal Opinions and Advice, 1807–1825.
M1029.   1 roll.   DP.

Letters Sent by the Secretary of the Navy to Officers, 1798–1868.
M149.   86 rolls.   DP.

Miscellaneous Letters Sent by the Secretary of the Navy, 1798–1886.
M209.   43 rolls.   DP.

Letters Sent by the Secretary of the Navy to Commandants and Navy Agents, 1808–1865.
M441.   5 rolls.   DP.

Letters Sent by the Secretary of the Navy to the President and Executive Agencies, 1821–1886.
M472.   20 rolls.   DP.

Letters Sent by the Secretary of the Navy to Chiefs of Navy Bureaus, 1842–1886.
M480.   3 rolls.   DP.

Correspondence of the Secretary of the Navy Relating to African Colonization, 1819–1844.
M205.   2 rolls.   DP.

Letters Sent by the War Department Relating to Naval Matters, Jan. 3, 1794–June 14, 1798.
M739.   1 roll.   DP.

Other Records

Records Relating to the U.S. Surveying Expedition to the North Pacific Ocean, 1852–1863.
M88.   27 rolls.   DP.

History of the Boston Navy Yard, 1797–1874, by Commodore George Henry Preble, U.S.N., 1875.
M118.   1 roll.   DP.

Papers of Stephen C. Rowan, 1826–1890.
M180.   1 roll.   DP.

Letter Books of Commodore Matthew C. Perry, 1843–1845.
M206.   1 roll.   DP.

Area File of the Naval Records Collection, 1775–1910.
M625.   414 rolls.   DP.

Journal of Lt. Charles Gauntt Aboard the U.S.S. *Macedonian*, 1818–1821.
M875.   1 roll.   DP.

Journal of Charles J. Deblois, Captain's Clerk, Aboard the U.S.S. *Macedonian*, 1818–1819.
M876.   1 roll.   DP.

Report of Capt. James Biddle, Commanding the U.S.S. *Ontario*, 1817–1819.
M902.   1 roll.   DP.

The Journals of Thomas A. Dornin, U.S. Navy, 1826–1855.
M981.   1 roll.   DP.

The Journal of Lt. Comdr. William B. Cushing, 1861–1865.
M1034.   1 roll.   DP.

Subject File of the Confederate States Navy, 1861–1865.
M1091.   61 rolls.   DP.

Journal of John Landreth on an Expedition to the Gulf Coast, Nov. 15, 1818–May 19, 1819.
T12.   1 roll.

Log of Arctic Steamer *Jeanette*.
T297.   1 roll.

Log of the U.S.S. *Nautilus* Aug. 1–31, 1958.
T319.   1 roll.

Private Journals of Commodore Matthew C. Perry, 1853–1854.
T1097.   1 roll.

Records of the U.S. Senate. RG 46

Territorial Papers of the U.S. Senate, 1789–1873.
M200.   20 rolls.   DP.

Records of the Senate Select Committee That Investigated John Brown's Raid at Harper's Ferry, Virginia, in 1859.
M1196.   3 rolls.   DP.

Journal of the Legislative Proceedings of the U.S. Senate, 1789–1817.
M1251.   28 rolls.   DP.

Journal of the Executive Proceedings of the U.S. Senate, 1789–1823.
M1252.   3 rolls.   DP.

Journal of the Impeachment Proceedings Before the U.S. Senate, 1798–1805.
M1253.   1 roll.   DP.

Journal of the Secretary of the Senate, 1789–1845.
M1254.   1 roll.   DP.

Bill Books of the U.S. Senate, 1795–1845.
M1255.   2 rolls.   DP.

Transcribed Reports of Committees of the U.S. Senate, 1817–1827.
M1256.   2 rolls.   DP.

Transcribed Reports and Communications Transmitted by the Executive Branch to the U.S. Senate, 1789–1819, and Transcribed Reports of Senate Committees, 1798–1817.
M1257.   4 rolls.   DP.

Transcribed Treaties and Conventions Approved by the U.S. Senate, 1789–1836.
M1258.   2 rolls.   DP.

Registers of Documents Presented to the U.S. Senate, 1814–1828.
M1259.   1 roll.   DP.

Engrossed Bills and Resolutions of the U.S. Senate, 1789–1817.
M1260.   5 rolls.   DP.

Register of Credentials of U.S. Senators, 1789–1821.
M1261.   1 roll.   DP.

➤Petitions Submitted to the U.S. Senate Requesting the Removal of Political Disabilities of Former Confederate Officeholders, 1869–1877.
M1546.   14 rolls.   DP.

➤Unbound Records of the U.S. Senate, Fifth Congress, 1797–1799.
M1704.   5 rolls.   DP.

➤Unbound Records of the U.S. Senate, Sixth Congress, 1799–1801.
M1706.   8 rolls.   DP.

Unbound Records of the U.S. Senate for the Eighth Congress, 1803–1805.
M1403.   5 rolls.   DP.

Records of the Office of the Secretary of the Interior. RG 48

Territorial Papers

Interior Department Territorial Papers: Alaska, 1869–1911.
M430.   17 rolls.   DP.

Interior Department Territorial Papers: Arizona, 1868–1913.
M429.   8 rolls.   DP.

Interior Department Territorial Papers: Colorado, 1861–1888.
M431.   1 roll.   DP.

Interior Department Territorial Papers: Dakota, 1863–1889.
M310.   3 rolls.   DP.

Interior Department Territorial Papers: Hawaii, 1898–1907.
M827.   4 rolls.   DP.

Interior Department Territorial Papers: Idaho, 1864–1890.
M191.   3 rolls.   DP.

Interior Department Territorial Papers: Montana, 1867–1889.
M192.　2 rolls.　DP.

Interior Department Territorial Papers: New Mexico, 1851–1914.
M364.　15 rolls.　DP.

Interior Department Territorial Papers: Oklahoma, 1889–1912.
M828.　5 rolls.　DP.

Interior Department Territorial Papers: Utah, 1850–1902.
M428.　6 rolls.　DP.

Interior Department Territorial Papers: Washington, 1854–1902.
M189.　4 rolls.　DP.

Interior Department Territorial Papers: Wyoming, 1870–1890.
M204.　6 rolls.　DP.

Appointment Papers

Interior Department Appointment Papers: Alaska, 1871–1907.
M1245.　6 rolls.　DP.

Interior Department Appointment Papers: Territory of Arizona, 1857–1907.
M576.　22 rolls.　DP.

Interior Department Appointment Papers: California, 1849–1907.
M732.　29 rolls.　DP.

Interior Department Appointment Papers: Territory of Colorado, 1857–1907.
M808.　13 rolls.　DP.

Interior Department Appointment Papers: Florida, 1849–1907.
M1119.　6 rolls.　DP.

Interior Department Appointment Papers: Idaho, 1862–1907.
M693.　17 rolls.　DP.

Interior Department Appointment Papers: Mississippi, 1849–1907.
M849.　4 rolls.　DP.

Interior Department Appointment Papers: Missouri, 1849–1907.
M1058.　9 rolls.　DP.

Interior Department Appointment Papers: Nevada, 1860–1907.
M1033.　3 rolls.　DP.

Interior Department Appointment Papers: Territory of New Mexico, 1850–1907.
M750.　18 rolls.　DP.

Interior Department Appointment Papers: New York, 1849–1906.
M1022.　5 rolls.　DP.

Interior Department Appointment Papers: North Carolina, 1849–1892.
M950.　1 roll.　DP.

Interior Department Appointment Papers: Territory of Oregon, 1849–1907.
M814.　10 rolls.　DP.

Interior Department Appointment Papers: Territory of Wisconsin, 1849–1907.
M831.　9 rolls.　DP.

Interior Department Appointment Papers: Wyoming, 1869–1907.
M830.　6 rolls.　DP.

Other Records

Records of the Office of the Secretary of the Interior Relating to Yellowstone National Park, 1872–1886.
M62.　6 rolls.　DP.

Records of the Office of the Secretary of the Interior Relating to Wagon Roads, 1857–1887.
M95.　16 rolls.　DP.

Correspondence of the Office of Explorations and Surveys Concerning Isaac Stevens' Survey of a Northern Route for the Pacific Railroad, 1853–1861.
M126.　1 roll.

Records of the Office of the Secretary of the Interior Relating to the Suppression of the African Slave Trade and Negro Colonization, 1854–1872.
M160.　10 rolls.　DP.

Letters Sent by the Indian Division of the Office of the Secretary of the Interior, 1849–1903.
M606.　127 rolls.　DP
See also: Records of the Bureau of Indian Affairs

Letters Sent by the Lands and Railroads Division of the Office of the Secretary of the Interior, 1849–1904.
M620.　310 rolls.　DP.

Letters Received by the Patents and Miscellaneous Division of the Office of the Secretary of the Interior Relating to Cuba, the Philippine Islands, and Puerto Rico, 1898–1907.
M824.　2 rolls.　DP.

Selected Classes of Letters Received by the Indian Division of the Office of the Secretary of the Interior, 1849–1880.
M825.　32 rolls.　DP.
See also: Records of the Bureau of Indian Affairs

Final Rolls of Citizens and Freedmen of the Five Civilized Tribes in Indian Territory (as Approved by the Secretary of the Interior on or Before Mar. 4, 1907, With Supplements Dated Sept. 25, 1914).
T529.　3 rolls.

Records of the Bureau of Land Management. RG 49

Journal and Report of James L. Cathcart and James Hutton, Agents Appointed by the Secretary of the Navy to Survey Timber Resources Between the Mermentau and Mobile Rivers, 1818–1819.
M8.　1 roll.　DP.

Miscellaneous Letters Sent by the General Land Office, 1796–1889.
M25.　228 rolls.　DP.

Letters Sent by the General Land Office to the Surveyor General, 1796–1901.
M27.　31 rolls.　DP.

List of North Carolina Land Grants in Tennessee, 1778–1791.
M68.　1 roll.　DP.

Abstracts of Oregon Donation Land Claims, 1852–1903.
M145.　6 rolls.　DP.

Abstracts of Washington Donation Land Claims, 1855–1902.
M203.　1 roll.　DP.

Letters Sent by the Surveyor General of the Territory Northwest of the Ohio River, 1797–1854.
M477.　10 rolls.　DP.

Letters Received by the Secretary of the Treasury and the Commissioner of the General Land Office From the Surveyor General of the Territory Northwest of the River Ohio, 1797–1849.
M478.　10 rolls.　DP.

Letters Received by the Surveyor General of the Territory Northwest of the River Ohio, 1797–1856.
M479.　43 rolls.　DP.

Oregon and Washington Donation
Land Files, 1851–1903.
M815.   108 rolls.   DP.

War of 1812 Military Bounty Land
Warrants, 1815–1858.
M848.   14 rolls.   DP.

U.S. Revolutionary War Bounty Land
Warrants Used in the U.S. Military
District of Ohio and Related Papers
(Acts of 1788, 1803, and 1806).
M829.   16 rolls.   DP.5.

Correspondence of the Surveyors
General of Utah, 1874–1916.
M1110.   86 rolls.   DP.

Correspondence Received by the
Surveyors General of New Mexico,
1854–1907.
M1288.   11 rolls.

Letters and Surveying Contracts
Received by the General Land Office
from the Surveyor General for Illinois,
Missouri, and Arkansas, 1813–1832.
M1323.   2 rolls.

Letters and Surveying Contracts
Received by the General Land Office
from the Surveyor General for
Alabama, 1817–1832.
M1325.   1 roll.

Letters Received by the Secretary of
the Treasury and the General Land
Office from the Surveyor General for
Mississippi, 1803–1831.
M1329.   4 rolls.1.

Bound Records of the General Land
Office Relating to Private Land Claims
in Louisiana, 1767–1892.
M1382.   8 rolls.   DP.

Unbound Records of the General Land
Office Relating to Private Land Claims
in Louisiana, 1805–1896.
M1385.   2 rolls.   DP.

Federal Land Records for Idaho,
1860–1934.
M1620.   23 rolls.

➤Federal Land Records for Oregon.
M1621.   93 rolls.

➤Federal Land Records for
Washington, 1860–1910.
M1622.   72 rolls.

➤Records of the Bureau of Land
Management, Surveyor General of
Arizona, 1891–1950.
M1627.   2 rolls.

➤Records of the Bureau of Land
Management, Phoenix General Land
Office, 1873–1942.
M1628.   15 rolls.

➤Records of the Bureau of Land
Management, Prescott General Land
Office, 1871–1908.
M1629.   16 rolls.

➤Records of the Bureau of Land
Management, Los Angeles District
Land Office, 1859–1936.
M1630.   60 rolls.

Register of Army Land Warrants
Issued Under the Act of 1788, for
Service in the Revolutionary War:
Military District of Ohio.
T1008.   1 roll.

Records of the General Land Office
Forest Lieu Selection Docket
Registers.
T1169.   6 rolls.

Township Plats of Selected States.
T1234.   67 rolls.

Field Notes From Selected General
Land Office Township Surveys.
T1240.   280 rolls.

Records of the Bureau of the Public Debt. RG 53

Records of the Bureau of the Public
Debt: Connecticut Loan Office
Records Relating to the Loan of 1790.
T654.   10 rolls.

Records of the Bureau of the Public
Debt: Delaware Loan Office Records
Relating to the Loan of 1790.
T784.   1 roll.

Records of the Delaware and
Maryland Continental Loan Office,
1777–1790.
M1008.   1 roll.   DP.

Records of the Bureau of the Public
Debt: Georgia Loan Office Records
Relating to the Loan of 1790.
T694.   2 rolls.

Records of the Bureau of the Public
Debt: Georgia Loan Office Records
Relating to Various Loans, 1804–1818.
T788.   1 roll.

Records of the Bureau of the Public
Debt: Maryland Loan Office Records
Relating to the Loan of 1790.
T697.   9 rolls.

Records of the Bureau of the Public Debt:
Maryland Loan Office Records Relating
to Various Loans of 1798 and 1800.
T957.   1 roll.

Records of the Bureau of the Public
Debt: Massachusetts Loan Office
Records Relating to the Loan of 1790.
T783.   7 rolls.

Records of the Massachusetts
Continental Loan Office, 1777–1791.
M925.   4 rolls.   DP.

Records of the Bureau of the Public
Debt: New Hampshire Loan Office
Records Relating to the Loan of 1790.
T652.   6 rolls.

Records of the Connecticut, New
Hampshire, and Rhode Island
Continental Loan Offices, 1777–1791.
M1005.   2 rolls.   DP.

Records of the Bureau of the Public
Debt: New Jersey Loan Office Records
Relating to the Loan of 1790.
T698.   2 rolls.

Records of the New Jersey and New York
Continental Loan Offices, 1777–1790.
M1006.   2 rolls.   DP.

Records of the Bureau of the Public
Debt: North Carolina Loan Office
Records Relating to the Loan of 1790.
T695.   4 rolls.

Records of the Bureau of the Public
Debt: Pennsylvania Loan Office
Records Relating to the Loan of 1790.
T631.   8 rolls.

Records of the Pennsylvania
Continental Loan Office, 1776–1788.
M1007.   3 rolls.   DP.

Records of the Bureau of the Public
Debt: Rhode Island Loan Office
Records Relating to the Loan of 1790.
T653.   13 rolls.

Records of the Bureau of the Public
Debt: South Carolina Loan Office
Records Relating to the Loan of 1790.
T719.   3 rolls.

Records of the Bureau of the Public
Debt: Virginia Loan Office Records
Relating to the Loan of 1790.
T696.   12 rolls.

Card Index to "Old Loan" Ledgers of
the Bureau of the Public Debt,
1790–1836.
M521.   15 rolls.   DP.   16mm.

Records of the Bureau of the Public Debt: Central Treasury Records Relating to the Loan of 1790.
T786.   1 roll.

Records of the Bureau of the Public Debt: Old Loans Records Relating to Selected Loans of the Period 1795–1807.
T787.   6 rolls.

Records of the Bureau of Plant Industry, Soils, and Agricultural Engineering. RG 54

Expedition Reports of the Office of Foreign Seed and Plant Introduction of the Department of Agriculture, 1900–1938.
M840.   38 rolls.   DP.

Records of the Government of the Virgin Islands. RG 55

Customs Journals of the Danish Government of the Virgin Islands.
T39.   22 rolls.

Records Relating to the Danish West Indies, 1672–1860, Received From the Danish National Archives.
T952.   19 rolls.

General Records of the Department of the Treasury. RG 56

Records of the Commissioners of Claims (Southern Claims Commission), 1871–1880.
M87.   14 rolls.   DP.

Letters Received by the Secretary of the Treasury From Collectors of Customs ("G", "H", "I" Series), 1833–1869.
M174.   226 rolls.   DP.

Letters Sent by the Secretary of the Treasury to Collectors of Customs at All Ports, 1789–1847, and at Small Ports, 1847–1878 ("G" Series).
M175.   43 rolls.   DP.

Letters Sent by the Secretary of the Treasury to the Collectors of Customs at Baltimore, Boston, New Orleans, and Philadelphia ("I" Series), 1847–1878.
T1257.   19 rolls.

Letters Sent by the Secretary of the Treasury to the Collectors of Customs at New York, ("H" Series), 1847–1878.
T1258.   30 rolls.

Letters Sent by the Secretary of the Treasury to Collectors of Customs at Pacific Ports ("J" Series), 1850–1878.
M176.   10 rolls.   DP.

Correspondence of the Secretary of the Treasury With Collectors of Customs, 1789–1833.
M178.   39 rolls.   DP.

Letters Received by the Secretary of the Treasury From Collectors of Customs at Port Townsend, Washington, Relating to Nominations for Office, 1865–1910.
M188.   14 rolls.   DP.

Letters Sent to the President by the Secretary of the Treasury ("A" Series), 1833–1878.
M415.   1 roll.

Registers of Letters Relating to Claims Received in the Office of the Secretary of the Treasury, 1864–1887.
M502.   2 rolls.   DP.

Letters Relating to Claims Received in the Office of the Secretary of the Treasury, 1864–1887.
M503.   91 rolls.   DP.

Letters Sent by the Secretary of the Treasury Relating to Restricted Commercial Intercourse ("BE" Series), 1861–1887.
M513.   8 rolls.   DP.

Treasury Department Papers Relating to the Louisiana Purchase.
T712.   1 roll.

Letters Received by the Secretary of the Treasury Relating to Public Lands ("N" Series), 1831–1849.
M726.   23 rolls.   DP.

Letters Sent by the Secretary of the Treasury Relating to Public Lands ("N" Series), 1801–1878.
M733.   4 rolls.   DP.

Circular Letters of the Secretary of the Treasury ("T" Series), 1789–1878.
M735.   5 rolls.   DP.

Letters Received by the Secretary of the Treasury Relating to the Subtreasury System ("U" Series), 1846–1860.
M736.   23 rolls.   DP.

Letters Sent by the Secretary of the Treasury Relating to the Subtreasury System ("U" Series), 1840–1878.
M737.   7 rolls.   DP.

Telegrams Sent by the Secretary of the Treasury ("XA" Series), 1850–1874.
M738.   3 rolls.   DP.

Miscellaneous Letters Sent by the Secretary of the Treasury, 1870–1887, and by the Assistant Secretary, 1876–1893.
M741.   4 rolls.   DP.

Correspondence of the Secretary of the Treasury Relating to the Administration of Trust Funds for the Chickasaw and Other Tribes ("S" Series), 1834–1872.
M749.   1 roll.   DP.

Records of the U.S. Geological Survey. RG 57

Letters Sent by the U.S. Geological Survey, 1879–1895.
M152.   29 rolls.   DP.

Letters Received by John Wesley Powell, Director of the Geographical and Geological Survey of the Rocky Mountain Region, 1869–1879.
M156.   10 rolls.   DP.

Registers of Letters Received by the U.S. Geological Survey, 1879–1901.
M157.   16 rolls.   DP.

Letters Received by the U.S. Geological Survey, 1879–1901.
M590.   118 rolls.   DP.

Records of the Geological Exploration of the Fortieth Parallel ("King Survey"), 1867–1881.
M622.   3 rolls.   DP.

Records of the Geological and Geographical Survey of the Territories ("Hayden Survey"), 1867–1879.
M623.   21 rolls.   DP.

Geological Survey and Marine Corps Surveys and Maps of the Dominican Republic, 1919–1923.
T282.   6 rolls.

Records of the Internal Revenue Service. RG 58

Internal Revenue Assessment Lists

Internal Revenue Assessment Lists for
Alabama, 1865–1866.
M754. 6 rolls. DP.

Internal Revenue Assessment Lists for
Arkansas, 1865–1866.
M755. 2 rolls. DP.

Internal Revenue Assessment Lists for
Arkansas, 1867–1874.
T1208. 4 rolls.

Internal Revenue Assessment Lists for
California, 1862–1866.
M756. 33 rolls. DP.

Internal Revenue Assessment Lists for
the Territory of Colorado, 1862–1866.
M757. 3 rolls. DP.

Internal Revenue Assessment Lists for
Connecticut, 1862–1866.
M758. 23 rolls. DP.

Internal Revenue Assessment Lists for
Delaware, 1862–1866.
M759. 8 rolls. DP.

Internal Revenue Assessment Lists for
the District of Columbia, 1862–1866.
M760. 8 rolls. DP.

Internal Revenue Assessment Lists for
Florida, 1865–1866.
M761. 1 roll. DP.

Internal Revenue Assessment Lists for
Georgia, 1865–1866.
M762. 8 rolls. DP.

Internal Revenue Assessment Lists for
the Territory of Idaho, 1865–1866.
M763. 1 roll. DP.

Internal Revenue Assessment Lists for
the Territory of Idaho, 1867–1874.
T1209. 1 roll.

Internal Revenue Assessment Lists for
Illinois, 1862–1866.
M764. 63 rolls.1 DP.

Internal Revenue Assessment Lists for
Indiana, 1862–1866.
M765. 42 rolls. DP.

Internal Revenue Assessment Lists for
Iowa, 1862–1866.
M766. 16 rolls. DP.

Internal Revenue Assessment Lists for
Kansas, 1862–1866.
M767. 3 rolls. DP.

Internal Revenue Assessment Lists for
Kentucky, 1862–1866.
M768. 24 rolls. DP.

Internal Revenue Assessment Lists for
Louisiana, 1863–1866.
M769. 10 rolls. DP.

Internal Revenue Assessment Lists for
Maine, 1862–1866.
M770. 15 rolls. DP.

Internal Revenue Assessment Lists for
Maryland, 1862–1866.
M771. 21 rolls. DP.

Internal Revenue Assessment Lists for
Michigan, 1862–1866.
M773. 15 rolls. DP.5.

Internal Revenue Assessment Lists for
Minnesota, 1862–1866.
M774. 3 rolls DP.

Internal Revenue Assessment Lists for
Mississippi, 1865–1866.
M775. 3 rolls. DP.6.

Internal Revenue Assessment Lists for
Missouri, 1862–1865.
M776. 22 rolls. DP.

Internal Revenue Assessment Lists for
Montana, 1864–1872.
M777. 1 roll. DP.

Internal Revenue Assessment Lists for
Nevada, 1863–1866.
M779. 2 rolls. DP.

Internal Revenue Assessment Lists for
New Hampshire, 1862–1866.
M780. 10 rolls. DP.

Internal Revenue Assessment Lists for
the Territory of New Mexico, 1862–
1870, 1872–1874.
M782. 1 roll. DP.

Internal Revenue Assessment Lists for
New York and New Jersey, 1862–
1866.
M603. 218 rolls.

Internal Revenue Assessment Lists for
North Carolina, 1864–1866.
M784. 2 rolls. DP.

➤Internal Revenue Assessment Lists,
Oregon District, 1867–73.
M1631. 2 rolls.

Internal Revenue Assessment Lists for
Pennsylvania, 1862–1866.
M787. 107 rolls. DP.

Internal Revenue Assessment Lists for
Rhode Island, 1862–1866.
M788. 10 rolls. DP.

Internal Revenue Assessment Lists for
South Carolina, 1864–1866.
M789. 2 rolls. DP.

Internal Revenue Assessment Lists for
Texas, 1865–1866.
M791. 2 rolls. DP.

Internal Revenue Assessment Lists for
Vermont, 1862–1866.
M792. 7 rolls. DP.

Internal Revenue Assessment Lists for
Virginia, 1862–1866.
M793. 6 rolls. DP.

Internal Revenue Assessment Lists for
West Virginia, 1862–1866.
M795. 4 rolls. DP.

Other Records

U.S. Direct Tax of 1798: Tax Lists for
the State of Pennsylvania.
M372 24 rolls. DP.

Letters Sent by the Commissioner of
the Revenue and the Revenue Office,
1792–1807.
M414. 3 rolls. DP.

Corporation Assessment Lists,
1909–1915.
M667. 82 rolls. DP.

General Records of the Department of State. RG 59

Diplomatic and Consular Instructions

Foreign Letters of the Continental
Congress and the Department of
State, 1785–1790.
M61. 1 roll. DP.

Diplomatic and Consular Instructions
of the Department of State,
1791–1801.
M28. 5 rolls. DP.

Diplomatic Instructions of the
Department of State, 1801–1906.
M77. 175 rolls. DP.

Consular Instructions of the
Department of State, 1801–1834.
M78.   7 rolls.

Diplomatic Despatches

Despatches From U.S. Ministers to
Argentina, 1817–1906.
M69.   40 rolls.   DP.

Despatches From U.S. Ministers to
Austria, 1838–1906.
T157.   51 rolls.

Despatches From U.S. Ministers to
Belgium, 1832–1906.
M193.   37 rolls.

Despatches From U.S. Ministers to
Bolivia, 1848–1906.
T51.   22 rolls.

Despatches From U.S. Ministers to
Brazil, 1809–1906.
M121.   74 rolls.   DP.

Despatches From U.S. Ministers to
Central America, 1824–1906.
M219.   93 rolls.

Despatches From U.S. Ministers to
Chile, 1823–1906.
M10.   52 rolls.

Despatches From U.S. Ministers to
China, 1843–1906.
M92.   131 rolls.   DP.

Despatches From U.S. Ministers to
Colombia, 1820–1906.
T33.   64 rolls.

Despatches From U.S. Ministers to
Cuba, 1902–1906.
T158.   18 rolls.

Despatches From U.S. Ministers to
Denmark, 1811–1906.
M41.   28 rolls.

Despatches From U.S. Ministers to the
Dominican Republic, 1883–1906.
M93.   15 rolls.

Despatches From U.S. Ministers to
Ecuador, 1848–1906.
T50.   19 rolls.

Despatches From U.S. Ministers to
France, 1789–1906.
M34.   128 rolls.

Despatches From U.S. Ministers to the
German States and Germany, 1799–
1801, 1835–1906.
M44.   107 rolls.   DP.

Despatches From U.S. Ministers to
Great Britain, 1791–1906.
M30.   200 rolls.   DP.

Despatches From U.S. Ministers to
Greece, 1868–1906.
T159.   18 rolls.

Despatches From U.S. Ministers to
Haiti, 1862–1906.
M82.   47 rolls.

Despatches From U.S. Ministers to
Hawaii, 1843–1900.
T30.   34 rolls.

Despatches From U.S. Ministers to the
Italian States, 1832–1906.
M90.   44 rolls.

Despatches From U.S. Ministers to
Japan, 1855–1906.
M133.   82 rolls.   DP.

Despatches From U.S. Ministers to
Korea, 1883–1905.
M134.   22 rolls.   DP.

Despatches From U.S. Ministers to
Liberia, 1863–1906.
M170.   14 rolls.

Despatches From U.S. Ministers to
Mexico, 1823–1906.
M97.   179 rolls.   DP.

Despatches From U.S. Ministers to
Montenegro, March 12, 1905–June 14,
1906.
T525.   1 roll.

Despatches From U.S. Ministers to
Morocco, 1905–1906.
T725.   1 roll.

Despatches From U.S. Ministers to
The Netherlands, 1794–1906.
M42.   46 rolls.

Despatches From U.S. Ministers to
Panama, 1903–1906.
T726.   5 rolls.

Despatches From U.S. Ministers to
Paraguay and Uruguay, 1858–1906.
M128.   19 rolls.

Despatches From U.S. Ministers to
Persia, 1883–1906.
M223.   11 rolls.   DP.

Despatches From U.S. Ministers to
Peru, 1826–1906.
T52.   66 rolls.

Despatches From U.S. Ministers to
Portugal, 1790–1906.
M43.   41 rolls.

Despatches From U.S. Ministers to
Rumania, 1880–1906.
T727.   5 rolls.

Despatches From U.S. Ministers to
Russia, 1808–1906.
M35.   66 rolls.

Despatches From U.S. Ministers to
Serbia, July 5, 1900–July 31, 1906.
T630.   1 roll.

Despatches From U.S. Ministers to
Siam, 1882–1906.
M172.   9 rolls.   DP.

Despatches From U.S. Ministers to
Spain, 1792–1906.
M31.   134 rolls.   DP.

Despatches From U.S. Ministers to
Sweden and Norway, 1813–1906.
M45.   28 rolls.

Despatches From U.S. Ministers to
Switzerland, 1853–1906.
T98.   35 rolls.

Despatches From U.S. Ministers to
Texas, 1836–1845.
T728.   2 rolls.

Despatches From U.S. Ministers to
Turkey, 1818–1906.
M46.   77 rolls.

Despatches From U.S. Ministers to
Venezuela, 1835–1906.
M79.   60 rolls.

Consular Despatches

Despatches From U.S. Consuls in
Aarau, Switzerland, 1898–1902.
T502.   1 roll.

Despatches From U.S. Consuls in
Acapulco, Mexico, 1823–1906.
M143.   8 rolls.   DP.

Despatches From U.S. Consuls in
Aden, Aden, 1880–1906.
T503.   3 rolls.

Despatches From U.S. Consuls in
Aguascalientes, Mexico, 1901–1906.
M285.   1 roll.   DP.

Despatches From U.S. Consuls in Aix-la-Chapelle, Germany, 1849–1906.
T356.　11 rolls.

Despatches From U.S. Consuls in Aleppo, Syria, 1835–1840.
T188.　1 roll.

Despatches From U.S. Consuls in Alexandretta, Turkey, 1896–1906.
T504.　1 roll.

Despatches From U.S. Consuls in Alexandria, Egypt, 1835–1873.
T45.　7 rolls.

Despatches From U.S. Consuls in Algiers, Algeria, 1785–1906.
M23.　19 rolls.

Despatches From U.S. Consuls in Alicante, Spain, 1788–1905.
T357.　3 rolls.

Despatches From U.S. Consuls in Altona, Germany, 1838–1869.
T358.　5 rolls.

Despatches From U.S. Consuls in Amapala, Honduras, 1873–1886.
See also Tegucigalpa, Honduras, 1871–1894 (Rolls 1–4).
T589.　1 roll.

Despatches From U.S. Consuls in Amherstburg, Canada, 1882–1906.
T590.　2 rolls.

Despatches From U.S. Consuls in Amoor River, Russia, 1856–1874.
T111.　2 rolls.

Despatches From U.S. Consuls in Amoy, China, 1844–1906.
M100.　15 rolls.

Despatches From U.S. Consuls in Amsterdam, The Netherlands, 1790–1906.
M446.　7 rolls.　DP.

Despatches From U.S. Consuls in Ancona, Italy, 1840–1874.
T359.　2 rolls.

Despatches From U.S. Consuls in Annaberg, Germany, 1882–1906.
T592.　3 rolls.

Despatches From U.S. Consuls in Antigua, Leeward Islands, British West Indies, 1794–1906.
T327.　9 rolls.

Despatches From U.S. Consuls in Antofagasta, Chile, 1893–1906.
T505.　1 roll.

Despatches From U.S. Consuls in Antung, Manchuria, China, 1904–1906.
M447.　1 roll.　DP.

Despatches From U.S. Consuls in Antwerp, Belgium, 1802–1906.
T181.　14 rolls.

Despatches From U.S. Consuls in Apia, Samoa, 1843–1906.
T27.　27 rolls.

Despatches From U.S. Consuls in Archangel, Russia, 1833–1861.
M481.　1 roll.　DP.

Despatches From U.S. Consuls in Arica, Chile, 1849–1906.
T328.　2 rolls.

Despatches From U.S. Consuls in Asuncion, Paraguay, 1844–1906.
T329.　6 rolls.

Despatches From U.S. Consuls in Athens, Greece, 1837–1906.
T362.　8 rolls.

Despatches From U.S. Consuls in Augsburg, Germany, 1846–1873.
See also Munich, Germany.
T361.　1 roll.

Despatches From U.S. Consuls in Aux Cayes, Haiti, 1797–1874.
T330.　4 rolls.

Despatches From U.S. Consuls in Baghdad, Iraq, 1888–1906.
T509.　2 rolls.

Despatches From U.S. Consuls in Bahia, Brazil, 1850–1906.
See also Sao Salvador, Brazil, for earlier despatches.
T331.　8 rolls.

Despatches From U.S. Consuls in Bamberg, Germany, 1892–1906.
See Munich, Germany, 1842–1845.
T510.　1 roll.

Despatches From U.S. Consuls in Bangkok, Siam, 1856–1906.
M448.　6 rolls.　DP.

Despatches From U.S. Consuls in Baracoa, Cuba, 1827–1846, 1878–1899.
T511.　3 rolls.

Despatches From U.S. Consuls in Barbados, British West Indies, 1823–1906.
T333.　17 rolls.

Despatches From U.S. Consuls in Barcelona, Spain, 1797–1906.
T121.　15 rolls.

Despatches From U.S. Consuls in Barmen, Germany, 1868–1906.
T363.　6 rolls.

Despatches From U.S. Consuls in Barranquilla, Colombia, 1883–1906.
See Sabanilla, Colombia, for earlier despatches.
T512.　6 rolls.

Despatches From U.S. Consuls in Basle, Switzerland, 1830–1906.
T364.　9 rolls.

Despatches From U.S. Consuls in Batavia, Java, Netherlands East Indies, 1818–1906.
M449.　6 rolls.　DP.

Despatches From U.S. Consuls in Bathurst, Gambia, British Africa, 1857–1889.
T365.　2 rolls.

Despatches From U.S. Consuls in Batum, Russia, 1890–1906.
M482.　1 roll.　DP.

Despatches From U.S. Consuls in Bay of Islands and Auckland, New Zealand, 1839–1906.
T49.　13 rolls.

Despatches From U.S. Consuls in Bayonne, France, 1835–1865.
T366.　1 roll.

Despatches From U.S. Consuls in Beirut, Lebanon, 1836–1906.
T367.　23 rolls.

Despatches From U.S. Consuls in Belfast, Ireland, 1796–1906.
T368.　11 rolls.

Despatches From U.S. Consuls in Belgrade, Serbia, 1883–1906.
T513.　1 roll.

Despatches From U.S. Consuls in Belize, British Honduras, 1847–1906.
T334.　8 rolls.

Despatches From U.S. Consuls in Belleville, Canada, 1878–1906.
T514.　2 rolls.

Despatches From U.S. Consuls in
Bergen, Norway, 1821–1906.
T369.   4 rolls.

Despatches From U.S. Consuls in
Berlin, Germany, 1865–1906.
T163.   27 rolls.

Despatches From U.S. Consuls in
Bermuda, British West Indies, 1818–
1906.
T262.   11 rolls.

Despatches From U.S. Consuls in
Bern, Switzerland, 1882–1906.
T528.   3 rolls.

Despatches From U.S. Consuls in
Bilbao, Spain, 1791–1875.
T183.   1 roll.

Despatches From U.S. Consuls in
Birmingham, England, 1869–1906.
T247.   6 rolls.

Despatches From U.S. Consuls in
Bogota, Colombia, 1851–1906.
T116.   4 rolls.

Despatches From U.S. Consuls in
Boma, Congo, 1888–1895.
T47.   1 roll.

Despatches From U.S. Consuls in
Bombay, India, 1838–1906.
M168.   8 rolls.   DP.

Despatches From U.S. Consuls in
Bordeaux, France, 1783–1906.
T164.   13 rolls.

Despatches From U.S. Consuls in
Boulogne, France, 1866–1874.
T413.   1 roll.

Despatches From U.S. Consuls in
Bradford, England, 1865–1906.
T165.   8 rolls.

Despatches From U.S. Consuls in
Bremen, Germany, 1794–1906.
T184.   21 rolls.

Despatches From U.S. Consuls in
Breslau, 1878–1906.
T532.   3 rolls.

Despatches From U.S. Consuls in
Brindisi, Italy, 1864–1876.
T370.   1 roll.

Despatches From U.S. Consuls in
Bristol, England, 1792–1906.
T185.   16 rolls.

Despatches From U.S. Consuls in
Brockville, Canada, 1885–1906.
T530.   1 roll.

Despatches From U.S. Consuls in
Brunei, Borneo, 1862–1868.
T110.   1 roll.

Despatches From U.S. Consuls in
Brunswick, Germany, 1858–1906.
T371.   6 rolls.

Despatches From U.S. Consuls in
Brusa (Brousa), Turkey, 1837–1840.
T711.   1 roll.

Despatches From U.S. Consuls in
Brussels, Belgium, 1863–1906.
T166.   4 rolls.

Despatches From U.S. Consuls in
Bucharest, Romania, 1866–1885,
1892–1906.
T285.   3 rolls.

Despatches From U.S. Consuls in
Budapest, Hungary, 1876–1906.
T531.   4 rolls.

Despatches From U.S. Consuls in
Buenaventura, Colombia, 1867–1885.
M140.   1 roll.

Despatches From U.S. Consuls in
Buenos Aires, Argentina, 1811–1906.
M70.   25 rolls.

Despatches From U.S. Consuls in
Burslem, England, 1905–1906.
T533.   1 roll.

Despatches From U.S. Consuls in
Butaritari, Gilbert Islands, 1888–1892.
T89.   1 roll.

Despatches From U.S. Consuls in
Cadiz, Spain, 1791–1904.
T186.   20 rolls.

Despatches From U.S. Consuls in
Cagliari, Italy, 1802–1825.
T187.   1 roll.

Despatches From U.S. Consuls in
Cairo, Egypt, 1864–1906.
T41.   24 rolls.

Despatches From U.S. Consuls in
Calais, France, 1804–1906.
T373.   1 roll.

Despatches From U.S. Consuls in
Calcutta, India, 1792–1906.
M450.   7 rolls.   DP.

Despatches From U.S. Consuls in
Callao, Peru, 1854–1906.
M155.   17 rolls.   DP.

Despatches From U.S. Consuls in
Camargo, Mexico, 1870–1880.
M288.   1 roll.   DP.

Despatches From U.S. Consuls in
Campbellton, Canada, 1897–1906.
T535.   1 roll.

Despatches From U.S. Consuls in
Campeche, Mexico, 1820–1880.
M286.   1 roll.   DP.

Despatches From U.S. Consuls in
Candia, Crete, 1836–1841.
T374.   1 roll.

Despatches From U.S. Consuls in
Canea, Crete, 1832–1874.
See also Cyprus.
T190.   2 rolls.

Despatches From U.S. Consuls in
Cannes, France, 1891.
T537.   1 roll.

Despatches From U.S. Consuls in
Canton, China, 1790–1906.
M101.   20 rolls.   DP.

Despatches From U.S. Consuls in
Cap Haitien, Haiti, 1797–1906.
M9.   17 rolls.

Despatches From U.S. Consuls in Cape
Gracias a Dios, Nicaragua, 1903–1906.
T538.   1 roll.

Despatches From U.S. Consuls in Cape
Town, Cape Colony, 1800–1906.
T191.   22 rolls.

Despatches From U.S. Consuls in
Caracas, Venezuela, 1868–1885.
T599.   1 roll.

Despatches From U.S. Consuls in
Cardenas, Cuba, 1843–1845,
1879–1898.
T583.   5 rolls.

Despatches From U.S. Consuls in
Cardiff, Wales, 1861–1906.
T375.   6 rolls.

Despatches From U.S. Consuls in
Carlisle, England, 1867–1869.
T639.   1 roll.

Despatches From U.S. Consuls in
Carlsbad, Czechoslovakia, 1902–1906.
T540.   1 roll.

Despatches From U.S. Consuls in
Carlsruhe, Germany, 1854–1874.
See Mannheim, Germany, for later
despatches.
T541.   3 rolls.

Despatches From U.S. Consuls in
Carrara, Italy, 1852–1881.
T376.   1 roll.

Despatches From U.S. Consuls in
Cartagena, Colombia, 1822–1906.
T192.   14 rolls.

Despatches From U.S. Consuls in
Cartagena, Spain, 1863–1906.
T377.   1 roll.

Despatches From U.S. Consuls in
Castellammare di Stabia, Italy, 1878–
1906.
T543.   3 rolls.

Despatches From U.S. Consuls in
Catania, Italy, 1883–1906.
T544.   4 rolls.

Despatches From U.S. Consuls in
Cayenne, French Guiana, 1801–1897.
T378.   1 roll.

Despatches From U.S. Consuls in
Ceiba, Honduras, 1902–1906.
See Tegucigalpa, Honduras, for earlier
despatches.
T545.   1 roll.

Despatches From U.S. Consuls in
Cette, France, 1802–1840.
T379.   1 roll.

Despatches From U.S. Consuls in
Charlottetown, Canada, 1857–1906.
See also Pictou, Canada.
T462.   5 rolls.

Despatches From U.S. Consuls in
Chatham, Canada, 1879–1906.
T546.   3 rolls.

Despatches From U.S. Consuls in
Chaudiere Junction, Canada, 1898–
1905.
T547.   1 roll.

Despatches From U.S. Consuls in
Chefoo, China, 1863–1906.
M102.   9 rolls.   DP.

Despatches From U.S. Consuls in
Chemnitz, Germany, 1867–1906.
T380.   8 rolls.

Despatches From U.S. Consuls in
Chihuahua, Mexico, 1830–1906.
M289.   3 rolls.   DP.

Despatches From U.S. Consuls in
Chinkiang, China, 1864–1902.
See Nanking, China, for later
despatches.
M103.   7 rolls.

Despatches From U.S. Consuls in
Chios, Greece, 1862–1871.
T669.   1 roll.

Despatches From U.S. Consuls in
Christiania, Norway, 1869–1906.
T122.   5 rolls.

Despatches From U.S. Consuls in
Christiansand, Norway, 1810–1891.
T235.   1 roll.

Despatches From U.S. Consuls in
Chungking, China, 1896–1906.
M104.   1 roll.

Despatches From U.S. Consuls in
Cienfuegos, Cuba, 1876–1906.
See Trinidad, Cuba, for earlier
despatches.
T548.   8 rolls.

Despatches From U.S. Consuls in
Ciudad Bolivar, Venezuela, 1850–1893.
T335.   3 rolls.

Despatches From U.S. Consuls in
Ciudad del Carmen, Mexico, 1830–
1872.
M308.   1 roll.   DP.

Despatches From U.S. Consuls in
Ciudad Juarez (Paso del Norte),
Mexico, 1850–1906.
M184.   6 rolls.

Despatches From U.S. Consuls in
Clifton, Canada, 1864–1906.
T549.   7 rolls.

Despatches From U.S. Consuls in
Coaticook, Canada, 1864–1906.
T550.   4 rolls.

Despatches From U.S. Consuls in
Cobija, Bolivia, 1854–1874.
T381.   1 roll.

Despatches From U.S. Consuls in
Coburg, Germany, 1898–1906.
T551.   2 rolls.

Despatches From U.S. Consuls in
Cognac, France, 1883–1898.
See also La Rochelle, France.
T552.   2 rolls.

Despatches From U.S. Consuls in
Collingwood, Canada, 1879–1906.
T553.   3 rolls.

Despatches From U.S. Consuls in
Cologne, Germany, 1876–1906.
T555.   5 rolls.

Despatches From U.S. Consuls in
Colombo, Ceylon, 1850–1906.
M451.   4 rolls.   DP.

Despatches From U.S. Consuls in
Colon, Panama, 1852–1906.
T193   19 rolls.

Despatches From U.S. Consuls in
Colonia, Uruguay, 1870–1906.
T556.   1 roll.

Despatches From U.S. Consuls in
Constantinople, Turkey, 1820–1906.
T194.   24 rolls.

Despatches From U.S. Consuls in
Copenhagen, Denmark, 1792–1906.
T195.   11 rolls.

Despatches From U.S. Consuls in
Coquimbo, Chile, 1850–1898.
See Valparaiso, Chile, for later despatches.
T332.   1 roll.

Despatches From U.S. Consuls in
Cordoba, Argentina, 1870–1906.
T557.   1 roll.

Despatches From U.S. Consuls in Cork,
Ireland, 1800–1906.
T196.   12 rolls.

Despatches From U.S. Consuls in
Cornwall, Canada, 1901–1906.
See Morrisburg, Canada, for earlier
despatches.
T558.   2 rolls.

Despatches From U.S. Consuls in
Corunna, Spain, 1867–1906.
T450.   2 rolls.

Despatches From U.S. Consuls in
Crefeld, Germany, 1878–1906.
T559.   5 rolls.

Despatches From U.S. Consuls in Curacao,
Netherlands West Indies, 1793–1906.
T197.   13 rolls.

Despatches From U.S. Consuls in
Cyprus, 1835–1878.
T463.   2 rolls.

Despatches From U.S. Consuls in
Dawson City, Canada, 1898–1906.
T560.   4 rolls.

Despatches From U.S. Consuls in
Denia, Spain, 1852–1898.
T382.   2 rolls.

Despatches From U.S. Consuls in Dresden, Germany, 1837–1906. T383.　6 rolls.

Despatches From U.S. Consuls in Dublin, Ireland, 1790–1906. T199.　11 rolls.

Despatches From U.S. Consuls in Dundee, Scotland, 1834–1906. T200.　8 rolls.

Despatches From U.S. Consuls in Dunfermline, Scotland, 1877–1906. T561.　3 rolls.

Despatches From U.S. Consuls in Durango, Mexico, 1886–1906. M290.　1 roll.　DP.

Despatches From U.S. Consuls in Dusseldorf, Germany, 1881–1906. T562.　3 rolls.

Despatches From U.S. Consuls in Edinburgh, Scotland, 1893–1906. *See* Leith, Scotland, for earlier despatches. T602.　1 roll.

Despatches From U.S. Consuls in Eibenstock, Germany, 1902–1906. T565.　1 roll.

Despatches From U.S. Consuls in Elberfeld, Lubeck, and Rostock, Germany, 1804–1849, 1883–1889. T566.　1 roll.

Despatches From U.S. Consuls in Elsinore, Denmark, 1792–1874. T201.　6 rolls.

Despatches From U.S. Consuls in Ensenada, Mexico, 1888–1906. M291.　1 roll.　DP.

Despatches From U.S. Consuls in Erfurt, Germany, 1892–1894. T563.　1 roll.

Despatches From U.S. Consuls in Erzerum, Turkey, 1895–1904. T568.　2 rolls.

Despatches From U.S. Consuls in Falmouth, British West Indies, 1790–1905. T202.　12 rolls.

Despatches From U.S. Consuls in Fayal, Azores, Portugal, 1795–1897. *See also* St. Michael Island, Azores. T203.　11 rolls.

Despatches From U.S. Consuls in Florence, Italy, 1824–1906. T204.　10 rolls.

Despatches From U.S. Consuls in Foochow, China, 1849–1906. M105.　10 rolls.　DP.

Despatches From U.S. Consuls in Fort Erie, Canada, 1865–1906. T465.　3 rolls.

Despatches From U.S. Consuls in Frankfort on the Main, Germany, 1829–1906. M161.　30 rolls.

Despatches From U.S. Consuls in Freiburg, Germany, 1892–1906. T569.　2 rolls.

Despatches From U.S. Consuls in Funchal, Madeira, Portugal, 1793–1906. T205.　9 rolls.

Despatches From U.S. Consuls in Furth, Germany, 1890–1898. *See* Solingen, Germany, for later despatches. T689.　1 roll.

Despatches From U.S. Consuls in Gaboon, 1856–1888. T466.　1 roll.

Despatches From U.S. Consuls in Galatz, Romania, 1858–1869. *See also* Bucharest, Romania. T384.　1 roll.

Despatches From U.S. Consuls in Galveston, Texas, 1832–1846. *See also* Texas. T151.　2 rolls.

Despatches From U.S. Consuls in Galway, Ireland, 1834–1863. T570.　1 roll.

Despatches From U.S. Consuls in Garrucha, Spain, 1877–1897. T571.　1 roll.

Despatches From U.S. Consuls in Gaspe Basin, Canada, 1856–1906. T467.　6 rolls.

Despatches From U.S. Consuls in Geestemunde, Germany,1867–1882. *See also* Hanover, Germany. T385.　1 roll.

Despatches From U.S. Consuls in Geneva, Switzerland, 1855–1906. T387.　6 rolls.

Despatches From U.S. Consuls in Genoa, Italy, 1799–1906. T64.　13 rolls.

Despatches From U.S. Consuls in Georgetown, Demerara, British Guiana, 1827–1906. T336.　23 rolls.

Despatches From U.S. Consuls in Ghent, Belgium, 1860–1906. T388.　6 rolls.

Despatches From U.S. Consuls in Gibraltar, Spain, 1791–1906. T206.　17 rolls.

Despatches From U.S. Consuls in Glasgow, Scotland, 1801–1906. T207.　12 rolls.

Despatches From U.S. Consuls in Glauchau, Germany, 1891–1906. T572.　2 rolls.

Despatches From U.S. Consuls in Gloucester, England, 1879–1886. T539.　1 roll.

Despatches From U.S. Consuls in Goderich, Canada, 1865–1906. T468.　4 rolls.

Despatches From U.S. Consuls in Goree Dakar, French Africa, 1883–1906. T573.　2 rolls.

Despatches From U.S. Consuls in Gothenburg, Sweden, 1800–1906. T276.　4 rolls.

Despatches From U.S. Consuls in Grand Bassa, Liberia, 1868–1882. M171.　1 roll.

Despatches From U.S. Consuls in Grenoble, France, 1893–1906. T574.　1 roll.

Despatches From U.S. Consuls in Grenville, Canada, 1904–1906. T575.　1 roll.

Despatches From U.S. Consuls in Guadeloupe, French West Indies, 1802–1906. T208.　8 rolls.

Despatches From U.S. Consuls in Guam, 1854–1856. M1306.　1 roll.

Despatches From U.S. Consuls in Guatemala City, Guatemala, 1824–1906. T337.　15 rolls.

Despatches From U.S. Consuls in Guayaquil, Ecuador, 1826–1906.
T209.   13 rolls.

Despatches From U.S. Consuls in Guaymas, Mexico, 1832–1896.
M284.   5 rolls.   DP.

Despatches From U.S. Consuls in Guelph, Canada, 1883–1906.
T578.   2 rolls.

Despatches From U.S. Consuls in Guerrero, Mexico, 1871–1888.
M292.   1 roll.   DP.

Despatches From U.S. Consuls in Hakodate, Japan, 1856–1878.
See also Kanagawa, Japan.
M452.   1 roll.   DP.

Despatches From U.S. Consuls in Halifax, Canada, 1833–1906.
T469.   18 rolls.

Despatches From U.S. Consuls in Hamburg, Germany, 1790–1906.
T211.   35 rolls.

Despatches From U.S. Consuls in Hamilton, Canada, 1867–1906.
See also Montreal, Canada.
T470.   8 rolls.

Despatches From U.S. Consuls in Hangchow, China, 1904–1906.
M106.   1 roll.

Despatches From U.S. Consuls in Hankow, China, 1861–1906.
M107.   8 rolls.   DP.

Despatches From U.S. Consuls in Hanover, Germany, 1854–1867, 1893–1906.
T372.   2 rolls.

Despatches From U.S. Consuls in Harput, Turkey, 1895–1906.
T579.   1 roll.

Despatches From U.S. Consuls in Havana, Cuba, 1783–1906.
M899.   133 rolls.

Despatches From U.S. Consuls in Havre, France, 1789–1906.
T212.   21 rolls.

Despatches From U.S. Consuls in Helsingfors, Finland, 1851–1906.
M483.   1 roll.   DP.

Despatches From U.S. Consuls in Hermosillo, Mexico, 1905–1906.
M293.   1 roll.   DP.

Despatches From U.S. Consuls in Hesse-Cassel, Germany, 1835–1869.
T213.   3 rolls.

Despatches From U.S. Consuls in Hesse-Darmstadt, Germany, 1854–1871.
See Mayence, Germany, for later despatches.
T390.   4 rolls.

Despatches From U.S. Consuls in Hesse-Homburg, Germany, 1854–1866.
T391.   1 roll.

Despatches From U.S. Consuls in Hilo, Hawaii, 1853–1872.
See Honolulu, Hawaii, for earlier despatches.
T133.   4 rolls.

Despatches From U.S. Consuls in Hobart, Australia, 1842–1906.
See also Sydney, Australia.
T127.   4 rolls.

Despatches From U.S. Consuls in Hong Kong, 1844–1906.
M108.   21 rolls.   DP.

Despatches From U.S. Consuls in Honolulu, Hawaii, 1820–1903.
M144.   22 rolls.   DP.

Despatches From U.S. Consuls in Horgen, Switzerland, 1882–1898.
T591.   3 rolls.

Despatches From U.S. Consuls in Huddersfield, England, 1890–1906.
T593.   1 roll.

Despatches From U.S. Consuls in Hull, United Kingdom, 1879–1906.
See Leeds-Upon-Hull, England, for earlier despatches.
T594.   4 rolls.

Despatches From U.S. Consuls in Iloilo, Philippine Islands, 1878–1886.
See Manila, Philippine Islands, for later despatches.
T109.   1 roll.

Despatches From U.S. Consuls in Iquique, Chile, 1877–1906.
T595.   5 rolls.

Despatches From U.S. Consuls in Jalapa Enriquez, Mexico, 1905–1906.
M294.   1 roll.   DP.

Despatches From U.S. Consuls in Jerez de la Frontera, Spain, 1903–1906.
T596.   1 roll.

Despatches From U.S. Consuls in Jerusalem, Palestine, 1856–1906.
M453.   5 rolls.   DP.

Despatches From U.S. Consuls in Kanagawa, Japan, 1861–1897.
See Yokohama, Japan, for later despatches.
M135.   22 rolls.

Despatches From U.S. Consuls in Kehl, Germany, 1882–1906.
T597.   5 rolls.

Despatches From U.S. Consuls in Kingston, Canada, 1864–1906.
T472.   5 rolls.

Despatches From U.S. Consuls in Kingston, Jamaica, British West Indies, 1796–1906.
T31.   40 rolls.

Despatches From U.S. Consuls in Konigsberg, East Prussia, Germany, 1879–1881.
T598.   1 roll.

Despatches From U.S. Consuls in La Guaira, Venezuela, 1810–1906.
M84.   23 rolls.

Despatches From U.S. Consuls in Lahaina, Hawaii, 1850–1871.
See also Honolulu, Hawaii.
T101.   3 rolls.

Despatches From U.S. Consuls in Lambayeque, Peru, 1860–1888.
T393.   3 rolls.

Despatches From U.S. Consuls in La Paz, Bolivia, 1869–1901.
T338.   2 rolls.

Despatches From U.S. Consuls in La Paz, Mexico, 1855–1906.
M282.   5 rolls.   DP.

Despatches From U.S. Consuls in La Rochelle, France, 1794–1906.
See also Cognac, France.
T394.   8 rolls.

Despatches From U.S. Consuls in Lauthala, Fiji Islands, 1844–1890.
See Levuka, Fiji Islands, for later despatches.
T25.   7 rolls.

Despatches From U.S. Consuls in La Union, El Salvador, 1854–1887.
T395.   1 roll.

Despatches From U.S. Consuls in Leeds-Upon-Hull, England, 1797–1906.
T474.   14 rolls.

Despatches From U.S. Consuls in
Leghorn, Italy, 1793–1906.
T214.   10 rolls.

Despatches From U.S. Consuls in
Leipzig, Germany, 1826–1906.
T215.   12 rolls.

Despatches From U.S. Consuls in
Leith, Scotland, 1798–1893.
See Edinburgh, Scotland, for later
despatches.
T396.   8 rolls.

Despatches From U.S. Consuls in
Levuka and Suva, Fiji Islands,
1891–1906.
See Lauthala, Fiji Islands, for
earlier despatches.
T108.   1 roll.

Despatches From U.S. Consuls in
Liberec, Czechoslovakia,
1886–1906.
T664.   3 rolls.

Despatches From U.S. Consuls in
Liege, Belgium, 1863–1906.
T397.   6 rolls.

Despatches From U.S. Consuls in
Lima, Peru, 1823–1854.
See Callao, Peru, for later
despatches.
M154.   6 rolls.   DP.

Despatches From U.S. Consuls in
Limoges, France, 1887–1906.
T601.   4 rolls.

Despatches From U.S. Consuls in
Lindsay, Canada, 1891–1892.
T603.   1 roll.

Despatches From U.S. Consuls in
Lisbon, Portugal, 1791–1906.
See also Fayal, Azores, and
Oporto, Portugal.
T180.   11 rolls.

Despatches From U.S. Consuls in
Liverpool, England, 1790–1906.
M141.   55 rolls.

Despatches From U.S. Consuls in
London, England, 1790–1906.
T168.   64 rolls.

Despatches From U.S. Consuls in
London, Canada, 1885–1906.
T604.   2 rolls.

Despatches From U.S. Consuls in
Londonderry, Ireland, 1835–1876.
T216.   3 rolls.

Despatches From U.S. Consuls in
Lourenco Marques, Mozambique,
Portuguese Africa, 1854–1906.
T171.   6 rolls.

Despatches From U.S. Consuls in
Lucerne, Switzerland, 1902–1906.
T605.   1 roll.

Despatches From U.S. Consuls in
Ludwigshafen, Germany, 1858–1874.
See Carlsruhe, Germany, for earlier
despatches.
T585.   1 roll.

Despatches From U.S. Consuls in
Luxembourg, Luxembourg,
1893–1896.
T607.   1 roll.

Despatches From U.S. Consuls in
Lyon, France, 1829–1906.
T169.   14 rolls.

Despatches From U.S. Consuls in
Macao, China, 1849–1869.
See also Canton, China.
M109.   2 rolls.   DP.

Despatches From U.S. Consuls in
Madrid, Spain, 1882–1884,
1891–1906.
T632.   2 rolls.

Despatches From U.S. Consuls in
Magdeburg, Germany, 1890–1906.
T633.   2 rolls.

Despatches From U.S. Consuls in
Mahe, Seychelles Islands, Indian
Ocean, 1868–1888.
M454.   1 roll.   DP.

Despatches From U.S. Consuls in
Malaga, Spain, 1793–1906.
T217.   17 rolls.

Malagasy Republic.
See Tamatave, Madagascar.

Despatches From U.S. Consuls in
Malta, 1801–1906.
T218.   13 rolls.

Despatches From U.S. Consuls in
Managua, Nicaragua, 1884–1906.
T634.   5 rolls.

Despatches From U.S. Consuls in
Manchester, England, 1847–1906.
T219.   7 rolls.

Despatches From U.S. Consuls in
Manila, Philippine Islands, 1817–1899.
M455.   6 rolls.   DP.

Despatches From U.S. Consuls in
Mannheim, Germany, 1874–1906.
See Carlsruhe, Germany, for earlier
despatches.
T582.   7 rolls.

Despatches From U.S. Consuls in
Manzanillo, Cuba, 1844–1846.
T613.   1 roll.

Despatches From U.S. Consuls in
Manzanillo, Mexico, 1855–1906.
M295.   2 rolls.   DP.

Despatches From U.S. Consuls in
Maracaibo, Venezuela, 1824–1906.
T62.   20 rolls.

Despatches From U.S. Consuls in
Maranham (Maranhao), Brazil,
1817–1876.
See also Para, Brazil.
T398.   3 rolls.

Despatches From U.S. Consuls in
Marseilles, France, 1790–1906.
T220.   20 rolls.

Despatches From U.S. Consuls in
Matamoras, Mexico, 1826–1906.
See also Texas.
M281.   12 rolls.   DP.

Despatches From U.S. Consuls in
Matanzas, Cuba, 1820–1899.
T339.   17 rolls.

Despatches From U.S. Consuls in
Mayence, Germany, 1871–1906.
See Hesse-Darmstadt, Germany, for
earlier despatches.
T635.   7 rolls.

Despatches From U.S. Consuls in
Mazatlan, Mexico, 1826–1906.
M159.   7 rolls.   DP.

Despatches From U.S. Consuls in
Medellin, Colombia, 1859–1902.
T341.   1 roll.

Despatches From U.S. Consuls in
Melbourne, Australia, 1852–1906.
T102.   16 rolls.

Despatches From U.S. Consuls in
Merida, 1843–1897, and Progreso,
Mexico, 1897–1906.
See also Santa Fe, New Mexico.
M287.   4 rolls.   DP.

Despatches From U.S. Consuls in
Messina, Italy, 1822–1906.
T399.   7 rolls.

Despatches From U.S. Consuls in Mexico City, Mexico, 1822–1906.
M296. 15 rolls. DP.

Despatches From U.S. Consuls in Mier, Mexico, 1870–1878.
M297. 1 roll. DP.

Despatches From U.S. Consuls in Milan, Italy, 1874–1906.
T170. 4 rolls.

Despatches From U.S. Consuls in Minatitlan, Mexico, 1853–1881.
M298. 2 rolls. DP.

Despatches From U.S. Consuls in Moncton, Canada, 1885–1905.
T636. 2 rolls.

Despatches From U.S. Consuls in Monrovia, Liberia, 1852–1906.
See also Despatches From U.S. Ministers to Liberia.
M169. 7 rolls. DP.

Despatches From U.S. Consuls in Monterey, Upper California, 1834–1848.
M138. 1 roll.

Despatches From U.S. Consuls in Monterrey, Mexico, 1849–1906.
M165. 7 rolls. DP.

Despatches From U.S. Consuls in Montevideo, Uruguay, 1821–1906.
M71. 15 rolls.

Despatches From U.S. Consuls in Montreal, Canada, 1850–1906.
T222. 22 rolls.

Despatches From U.S. Consuls in Morrisburg, Canada, 1882–1901.
See Cornwall, Canada, for later despatches.
T637. 1 roll.

Despatches From U.S. Consuls in Moscow, Russia, 1857–1906.
M456. 2 rolls. DP.

Despatches From U.S. Consuls in Mukden, Manchuria, China, 1904–1906.
M457. 1 roll. DP.

Despatches From U.S. Consuls in Munich, Germany, 1833–1906.
T261. 13 rolls.

Despatches From U.S. Consuls in Muscat, Oman, 1880–1906.
See also Zanzibar, British Africa.
T638. 2 rolls.

Despatches From U.S. Consuls in Nagasaki, Japan, 1860–1906.
M131. 7 rolls.

Despatches From U.S. Consuls in Nanking, China, 1902–1906.
See Chinkiang, China, for earlier despatches.
M110. 1 roll.

Despatches From U.S. Consuls in Nantes, France 1790–1906.
T223. 8 rolls.

Despatches From U.S. Consuls in Naples, Italy, 1796–1906.
T224. 12 rolls.

Despatches From U.S. Consuls in Napoleon-Vendee, France, 1800–1870.
T415. 1 roll.

Despatches From U.S. Consuls in Duchy of Nassau, Germany, 1854–1869.
T473. 1 roll.

Despatches From U.S. Consuls in Nassau, British West Indies, 1821–1906.
T475. 24 rolls.

Despatches From U.S. Consuls in Newcastle, Australia, 1887–1906.
T92. 6 rolls.

Despatches From U.S. Consuls in Newcastle upon Tyne, England, 1854–1906.
T416. 10 rolls.

Despatches From U.S. Consuls in Newchwang, Manchuria, China, 1865–1906.
M115. 7 rolls. DP.

Despatches From U.S. Consuls in New Orleans, Louisiana, 1798–1807.
T225. 1 roll.

Despatches From U.S. Consuls in Nice, France, 1819–1906.
T417. 7 rolls.

Despatches From U.S. Consuls in Ningpo, China, 1853–1896.
M111. 7 rolls.

Despatches From U.S. Consuls in Nogales, Mexico, 1889–1906.
M283. 4 rolls. DP.

Despatches From U.S. Consuls in Nottingham, England, 1877–1906.
T641. 3 rolls.

Despatches From U.S. Consuls in Noumea, New Caledonia, 1887–1905.
T91. 2 rolls.

Despatches From U.S. Consuls in Novorossisk, Russia, 1883–1884.
M458. 1 roll. DP.

Despatches From U.S. Consuls in Nuernberg, Germany, 1846–1906.
T418. 9 rolls.

Despatches From U.S. Consuls in Nuevitas, Cuba, 1842–1847, 1892–1898.
T588. 1 roll.

Despatches From U.S. Consuls in Nuevo Laredo, Mexico, 1871–1906.
M280. 4 rolls. DP.

Despatches From U.S. Consuls in Oaxaca, Mexico, 1869–1878.
M328. 1 roll. DP.

Despatches From U.S. Consuls in Odessa, Russia, 1831–1906.
M459. 7 rolls. DP.

Despatches From U.S. Consuls in Oldenburg, Germany, 1856–1869.
T419. 2 rolls.

Despatches From U.S. Consuls in Omoa, Trujillo, and Roatan, Honduras, 1831–1893.
See Utila, Honduras, for later despatches.
T477. 6 rolls.

Despatches From U.S. Consuls in Oporto, Portugal, 1821–1877.
T342. 5 rolls.

Despatches From U.S. Consuls in Orillia, Canada, 1893–1906.
T642. 1 roll.

Despatches From U.S. Consuls in Osaka and Hiogo (Kobe), Japan, 1868–1906.
M460. 6 rolls. DP.

Despatches From U.S. Consuls in Otranto, Italy, 1861–1867.
T542. 1 roll.

Despatches From U.S. Consuls in Ottawa, Canada, 1877–1906.
T643. 12 rolls.

Despatches From U.S. Consuls in Pacang, Sumatra, Netherlands East Indies, 1853–1898.
See Batavia, Java, Netherlands East Indies for later despatches.
M461. 1 roll. DP.

Despatches From U.S. Consuls in Paita, Peru, 1833–1874.
T600.   3 rolls.

Despatches From U.S. Consuls in Palermo, Italy, 1803–1906.
T420.   11 rolls.

Despatches From U.S. Consuls in Palmerston, Canada, 1892–1900.
T647.   1 roll.

Despatches From U.S. Consuls in Panama City, Panama, 1823–1906.
M139.   27 rolls.

Despatches From U.S. Consuls in Para, Brazil, 1831–1906.
See also Maranham, Brazil.
T478.   9 rolls.

Despatches From U.S. Consuls in Paramaribo, Brazil, 1799–1897.
T226.   8 rolls.

Despatches From U.S. Consuls in Paris, France, 1790–1906.
T1.   32 rolls.

Despatches From U.S. Consuls in Patras, Greece, 1874–1906.
T648.   4 rolls.

Despatches From U.S. Consuls in Pernambuco, Brazil, 1817–1906.
T344.   17 rolls.

Despatches From U.S. Consuls in Peterborough, Canada, 1905–1906.
T649.   1 roll.

Despatches From U.S. Consuls in Petropavlovsk, Russia, 1875–1878.
T104.   1 roll.

Despatches From U.S. Consuls in Pictou, Canada, 1837–1897.
See Sydney, Canada, for later despatches.
T479.   6 rolls.

Despatches From U.S. Consuls in Piedras Negras, Mexico, 1868–1906.
M299.   5 rolls.   DP.

Despatches From U.S. Consuls in Piraeus, Greece, 1864–1874.
T534.   3 rolls.

Despatches From U.S. Consuls in Plauen, Germany, 1887–1906.
T536.   3 rolls.

Despatches From U.S. Consuls in Plymouth, England, 1793–1906.
T228.   7 rolls.

Despatches From U.S. Consuls in Ponape, Caroline Islands, 1890–1892.
T90.   1 roll.

Despatches From U.S. Consuls in Porsgrunn, Norway, 1861–1869.
T421.   1 roll.

Despatches From U.S. Consuls in Port Antonio, British West Indies, 1895–1906.
T650.   1 roll.

Despatches From U.S. Consuls in Port-au-Prince, Haiti, 1835–1906.
T346.   10 rolls.

Despatches From U.S. Consuls in Port Hope, Canada, 1882–1906.
T651.   2 rolls.

Despatches From U.S. Consuls in Port Limon, Costa Rica, 1902–1906.
T656.   1 roll.

Despatches From U.S. Consuls in Port Louis, Mauritius, Mascarene Islands, 1794–1805, 1817–1906.
M462.   8 rolls.   DP.

Despatches From U.S. Consuls in Port Mahon, Spain, 1803–1876.
T422.   4 rolls.

Despatches From U.S. Consuls in Porto Principe and Xibara, Cuba, 1828–1843.
T567.   1 roll.

Despatches From U.S. Consuls in Port Rowan, Canada, 1882–1906.
T657.   1 roll.

Despatches From U.S. Consuls in Port Said, Egypt, 1870–1876.
T658.   1 roll.

Despatches From U.S. Consuls in Port Stanley, Canada, and St. Thomas, Canada, 1878–1906.
T659.   4 rolls.

Despatches From U.S. Consuls in Port Stanley, Falkland Islands, 1851–1906.
T480.   4 rolls.

Despatches From U.S. Consuls in Prague, Czechoslovakia, 1869–1906.
T663.   4 rolls.

Despatches From U.S. Consuls in Prescott, Canada, 1864–1906.
T481.   5 rolls.

Despatches From U.S. Consuls in Pretoria, The Transvaal, 1898–1906.
T660.   3 rolls.

Despatches From U.S. Consuls in Puerto Cabello, Venezuela, 1823–1906.
T229.   12 rolls.

Despatches From U.S. Consuls in Puerto Cortes, Honduras, 1902–1906.
See Tegucigalpa, Honduras, for earlier despatches.
T661.   2 rolls.

Despatches From U.S. Consuls in Puerto Plata, Dominican Republic, 1875–1906.
T662.   3 rolls.

Despatches From U.S. Consular Representatives in Puerto Rico, 1821–1899.
M76.   31 rolls.

Despatches From U.S. Consuls in Quebec, Canada, 1861–1906.
See also Montreal, Canada.
T482.   7 rolls.

Letters Received by the Department of State From the Agent for Red River Affairs, 1867–1870.
See Winnipeg, Canada, for related despatches.
T23.   1 roll.

Despatches From U.S. Consuls in Reval, Estonia, 1859–1870.
M484.   1 roll.   DP.

Despatches From U.S. Consuls in Rheims, France, 1867–1906.
T424.   3 rolls.

Despatches From U.S. Consuls in Riga, Latvia, 1811–1872, 1890–1906.
See also St. Petersburg, Russia.
M485.   1 roll.   DP.

Despatches From U.S. Consuls in Rimouski, Canada, 1897–1906.
T666.   1 roll.

Despatches From U.S. Consuls in Rio de Janeiro, Brazil, 1811–1906.
T172.   33 rolls.

Despatches From U.S. Consuls in Rio Grande do Sul, Brazil, 1829–1897.
T145.   7 rolls.

Despatches From U.S. Consuls in Rio Macha, Colombia, 1835–1883.
T425.   1 roll.

Despatches From U.S. Consuls in Rome, Italy, 1801–1906.
T231.   20 rolls.

Despatches From U.S. Consuls in
Rosario, Argentina, 1858–1906.
T343.   3 rolls.

Despatches From U.S. Consuls in
Rotterdam, The Netherlands,
1802–1906.
T232.   13 rolls.

Despatches From U.S. Consuls in
Roubaix, France, 1890–1906.
T667.   2 rolls.

Despatches From U.S. Consuls in
Rouen, France, 1790, 1878–1906.
T668.   4 rolls.

Despatches From U.S. Consuls in
Sabanilla, Colombia, 1856–1884.
See Barranquilla, Colombia, for
earlier despatches.
T426.   5 rolls.

Despatches From U.S. Consuls in
Sagua la Grande, Cuba,
1878–1900.
T678.   6 rolls.

Despatches From U.S. Consuls in
Saigon, Vietnam, 1889–1906.
T103.   1 roll.

Despatches From U.S. Consuls in
St. Bartholomew, French West Indies,
1799–1899.
M72.   3 rolls.

Despatches From U.S. Consuls in
St. Christopher, West Indies
Federation, 1800–1906.
T234.   3 rolls.

Despatches From U.S. Consuls in
St. Croix, Virgin Islands, 1791–1876.
See also St. Thomas,
Virgin Islands.
T233.   8 rolls.

Despatches From U.S. Consuls in
St. Denis, Reunion Island, Mascarene
Islands, Indian Ocean, 1880–1892.
M463.   1 roll.   DP.

Despatches From U.S. Consuls in
St. Etienne, France, 1877–1906.
T672.   3 rolls.

Despatches From U.S. Consuls in
St. Eustatius, Netherlands West
Indies, 1793–1838.
T236.   1 roll.

Despatches From U.S. Consuls in
St. Gall, Switzerland, 1878–1906.
T673.   6 rolls.

Despatches From U.S. Consuls in St.
George, British West Indies, 1878–1906.
See also Bermuda, British West Indies.
T173.   1 roll.

Despatches From U.S. Consuls in St.
Helena, British West Africa, 1831–1906.
T428.   20 rolls.

Despatches From U.S. Consuls in St.
Hyacinthe, Canada, 1882–1906.
T674.   2 rolls.

Despatches From U.S. Consuls in St.
John, New Brunswick, Canada,
1835–1906.
T485.   10 rolls.

Despatches From U.S. Consuls in St.
John's, Newfoundland, Canada,
1852–1906.
See also Pictou, Canada.
T129.   9 rolls.

Despatches From U.S. Consuls in
St. Johns, Quebec, Canada,
1864–1906.
T484.   3 rolls.

Despatches From U.S. Consuls in
St. Marc, Haiti, 1861–1891.
T486.   1 roll.

Despatches From U.S. Consuls in
St. Martin, Netherlands West Indies,
1848–1906.
T429.   3 rolls.

Despatches From U.S. Consuls in
St. Michael Island, Azores, 1897–1906.
See also Fayal, Azores.
T675.   1 roll.

Despatches From U.S. Consuls in
St. Paul de Loanda, Portuguese Africa,
1854–1893.
See also Valencia, Spain.
T430.   5 rolls.

Despatches From U.S. Consuls in
St. Petersburg, Russia, 1803–1906.
M81.   18 rolls.   DP.

Despatches From U.S. Consuls in
St. Pierre, Martinique, French West
Indies, 1790–1906.
T431.   11 rolls.

Despatches From U.S. Consuls in
St. Pierre and Miquelon, 1850–1906.
T487.   4 rolls.

Despatches From U.S. Consuls in
St. Stephen, Canada, 1882–1906.
T676.   2 rolls.

Despatches From U.S. Consuls in St.
Thomas, Virgin Islands, 1804–1906.
T350.   17 rolls.

Despatches From U.S. Consuls in
St. Ubes, Portugal, 1835–1842.
T564. 1 roll.

Despatches From U.S. Consuls in
Salonica, Greece, 1832–1840.
T414.   1 roll.

Despatches From U.S. Consuls in
Saltillo, Mexico, 1876–1906.
M300.   1 roll.   DP.

Despatches From U.S. Consuls in
Samana, Dominican Republic,
1873–1905.
T670.   2 rolls.

Despatches From U.S. Consuls in
San Andres, Colombia, 1870–1878.
T554.   1 roll.

Despatches From U.S. Consuls in
San Blas, Mexico, 1837–1892.
M301.   1 roll.   DP.

Despatches From U.S. Consuls in
San Dimas, Mexico, 1871–1873.
M442.   1 roll.   DP.

Despatches From U.S. Consuls in
San Jose, Costa Rica, 1852–1906.
T35.   7 rolls.

Despatches From U.S. Consuls in San
Juan del Norte, Nicaragua, 1851–1906.
T348.   21 rolls.

Despatches From U.S. Consuls in
San Juan de los Remedios, Cuba,
1844–1846, 1879–1898.
T584.   2 rolls.

Despatches From U.S. Consuls in San
Juan del Sur, Nicaragua, 1847–1881.
T152.   4 rolls.

Despatches From U.S. Consuls in
San Luis Potosi, Mexico, 1869–1886.
M302.   1 roll.   DP.

Despatches From U.S. Consuls in
San Salvador, El Salvador, 1868–1906.
T237.   10 rolls.

Despatches From U.S. Consuls in
Santa Catarina, Brazil, 1831–1874.
T483.   2 rolls.

Despatches From U.S. Consuls in
Santa Fe, New Mexico, 1830–1846.
See also Merida, Mexico.
M199.   1 roll.   DP.

Despatches From U.S. Consuls in
Santa Marta, Colombia, 1823–1883.
T427.   2 rolls.

Despatches From U.S. Consuls in
Santander, Spain, 1862–1892.
T433.   1 roll.

Despatches From U.S. Consuls in
Santiago, Cape Verde Islands,
1818–1898.
T434.   7 rolls.

Despatches From U.S. Consuls in
Santiago de Cuba, Cuba, 1799–1906.
T55.   17 rolls.

Despatches From U.S. Consuls in
Santo Domingo, Dominican Republic,
1837–1906.
T56.   19 rolls.

Despatches From U.S. Consuls in
Santos, Brazil, 1831–1906.
T351.   6 rolls.

Despatches From U.S. Consuls in
Sao Salvador, Brazil, 1808–1849.
See Bahia, Brazil, for later despatches.
T432.   4 rolls.

Despatches From U.S. Consuls in Sarnia,
Canada, 1864–1906.
T488.   4 rolls.

Despatches From U.S. Consuls in
Sault Ste. Marie, Canada, 1891–1906.
T679.   1 roll.

Despatches From U.S. Consuls in
Schwerin, Germany, 1862–1869.
T435.   1 roll.

Despatches From U.S. Consuls in
Seoul, Korea, 1886–1906.
M167.   2 rolls.   DP.

Despatches From U.S. Consuls in
Seville, Spain, 1859–1906.
T436.   2 rolls.

Despatches From U.S. Consuls in
Shanghai, China, 1847–1906.
M112.   53 rolls.   DP.

Despatches From U.S. Consuls in
Sheffield, England, 1864–1906.
T248.   12 rolls.

Despatches From U.S. Consuls in
Sherbrooke, Canada, 1879–1906.
T680.   3 rolls.

Despatches From U.S. Consuls in Sierra
Leone, British Africa, 1858–1906.
T438.   5 rolls.

Despatches From U.S. Consuls in
Singapore, Straits Settlements, 1833–
1906.
M464.   16 rolls.   DP.

Despatches From U.S. Consuls in
Sivas, Turkey, 1886–1906.
T681.   2 rolls.

Despatches From U.S. Consuls in
Smyrna, Turkey, 1802–1906.
T238.   15 rolls.

Despatches From U.S. Consuls in
Sofia, Bulgaria, 1901–1904.
T682.   1 roll.

Despatches From U.S. Consuls in
Solingen, Germany, 1898–1905.
See Furth, Germany, for earlier
despatches.
T683.   2 rolls.

Despatches From U.S. Consuls in
Sonneberg, Germany, 1851–1898.
T439.   7 rolls.

Despatches From U.S. Consuls in
Sonsonate, El Salvador, 1868–1887.
T440.   1 roll.

Despatches From U.S. Consuls in
Sorel, Canada, 1882–1898.
T684.   1 roll.

Despatches From U.S. Consuls in
Southampton, England, 1790–1906.
T239.   10 rolls.

Despatches From U.S. Consuls in
Spezia, Italy, 1856–1869.
T441.   3 rolls.

Despatches From U.S. Consuls in
Stanbridge Station, Canada, 1878–1906.
T685.   2 rolls.

Despatches From U.S. Consuls in
Stavanger, Norway, 1905–1906.
T686.   1 roll.

Despatches From U.S. Consuls in
Stettin, Germany, 1830–1906.
T59.   10 rolls.

Despatches From U.S. Consuls in
Stockholm, Sweden, 1810–1906.
T230.   9 rolls.

Despatches From U.S. Consuls in
Strasbourg, France, 1866–1872.
T442.   1 roll.

Despatches From U.S. Consuls in
Stratford, Canada, 1887–1906.
T687.   2 rolls.

Despatches From U.S. Consuls in
Stuttgart, Germany, 1830–1906.
See also Carlsruhe, Germany.
T443.   8 rolls.

Despatches From U.S. Consuls in
Swansea, Wales, 1892–1906.
T688.   1 roll.

Despatches From U.S. Consuls in
Swatow, China, 1860–1881.
See also Canton, China.
M113.   4 rolls.

Despatches From U.S. Consuls in
Sydney, Australia, 1836–1906.
See also Hobart, Australia.
M173.   18 rolls.   DP.

Despatches From U.S. Consuls in
Sydney, Canada, 1838–1906.
See also Pictou, Canada.
T490.   2 rolls.

Despatches From U.S. Consuls in
Tabasco, Mexico, 1832–1874.
M303.   2 rolls.   DP.

Despatches From U.S. Consuls in
Tahiti, Society Islands, French Oceania,
1836–1906.
M465.   5 rolls.   DP.

Despatches From U.S. Consuls in
Talcahuano, Chile, 1836–1895.
See Valparaiso, Chile, for later despatches.
T115.   5 rolls.

Despatches From U.S. Consuls in
Tamatave, Madagascar, 1853–1906.
T60.   11 rolls.

Despatches From U.S. Consuls in
Tampico, Mexico, 1824–1906.
M304.   8 rolls.   DP.

Despatches From U.S. Consuls in
Tamsui, Formosa, 1898–1906.
M117.   1 roll.

Despatches From U.S. Consuls in
Tangier, Morocco, 1797–1906.
T61.   27 rolls.

Despatches From U.S. Consuls in
Taranto, Italy, 1861–1876.
T444.   1 roll.

Despatches From U.S. Consuls in
Tegucigalpa, Honduras, 1860–1906.
See Ceiba, Honduras, for later despatches.
T352.   8 rolls.

Despatches From U.S. Consuls in
Teheran, Iran, 1883–1906.
T305.   2 rolls.

Despatches From U.S. Consuls in Tehuantepec, Mexico, 1850–1867.
M305.   1 roll.   DP.

Despatches From U.S. Consuls in Teneriffe, Canary Islands, 1795–1906.
T690.   10 rolls.

Despatches From U.S. Consuls in Tetuan, Morocco, 1877–1888.
T156.   1 roll.

Despatches From U.S. Consuls in Texas, 1825–1844.
See also Galveston, Texas.
T153.   1 roll.

Despatches From U.S. Consuls in Three Rivers, Canada, 1881–1906.
T691.   3 rolls.

Despatches From U.S. Consuls in Tientsin, China, 1868–1906.
M114.   8 rolls.   DP.

Despatches From U.S. Consuls in Toronto, Canada, 1864–1906.
See also Montreal, Canada.
T491.   9 rolls.

Despatches From U.S. Consuls in Trebizond, Turkey, 1904–1906.
See also Constantinople, Turkey.
T700.   1 roll.

Despatches From U.S. Consuls in Trieste, Italy, 1800–1906.
T242.   13 rolls.

Despatches From U.S. Consuls in Trinidad, Cuba, 1824–1876.
See Cienfuegos, Cuba, for later despatches.
T699.   9 rolls.

Despatches From U.S. Consuls in Trinidad, West Indies Federation, 1824–1906.
T148.   11 rolls.

Despatches From U.S. Consuls in Tripoli, Libya, 1796–1885.
M466.   7 rolls.   DP.

Despatches From U.S. Consuls in Tumbes, Peru, 1852–1874.
T353.   2 rolls.

Despatches From U.S. Consuls in Tunis, Tunisia, 1797–1906.
T303.   12 rolls.

Despatches From U.S. Consuls in Tunstall, England, 1869–1905.
T445.   3 rolls.

Despatches From U.S. Consuls in Turin, Italy, 1877–1906.
T174.   2 rolls.

Despatches From U.S. Consuls in Turks Island, British West Indies, 1818–1906.
T446.   18 rolls.

Despatches From U.S. Consuls in Tuxpan, Mexico, 1879–1906.
M306.   2 rolls.   DP.

Despatches From U.S. Consuls in Utila, Honduras, 1894–1906.
See Omoa, Honduras, for earlier despatches.
T701.   2 rolls.

Despatches From U.S. Consuls in Valencia, Spain, 1816–1906.
See also Barcelona, Spain.
T447.   4 rolls.

Despatches From U.S. Consuls in Valparaiso, Chile, 1812–1906.
See Coquimbo, Chile, and Talcahuano, Chile, for earlier despatches.
M146.   14 rolls.   DP.

Despatches From U.S. Consuls in Vancouver, Canada, 1890–1906.
T114.   5 rolls.

Despatches From U.S. Consuls in Venice, Italy, 1830–1906.
M153.   7 rolls.

Despatches From U.S. Consuls in Veracruz, Mexico, 1822–1906.
M183.   18 rolls.   DP.

Despatches From U.S. Consuls in Victoria, Canada, 1862–1906.
T130.   16 rolls.

Despatches From U.S. Consuls in Vienna, Austria, 1830–1906.
See also Dresden, Germany.
T243.   20 rolls.

Despatches From U.S. Consuls in Vigo, Spain, 1852–1862
See Corunna, Spain, for later despatches.
T449.   1 roll.

Despatches From U.S. Consuls in Vladivostok, Russia, 1898–1906.
M486.   1 roll.   DP.

Despatches From U.S. Consuls in Wallaceburg, Canada, 1888–1905.
T702.   1 roll.

Despatches From U.S. Consuls in Warsaw, Poland, 1871–1906.
M467.   3 rolls.   DP.

Despatches From U.S. Consuls in Waubaushene, Canada, 1890–1893.
T704.   1 roll.

Despatches From U.S. Consuls in Weimar, Germany, 1893–1906.
T705.   1 roll.

Despatches From U.S. Consuls in Windsor, Nova Scotia, Canada, 1872–1906.
T706.   3 rolls.

Despatches From U.S. Consuls in Windsor, Ontario, Canada, 1864–1906.
T492.   4 rolls.

Despatches From U.S. Consuls in Winnipeg, Canada, 1869–1906.
See Red River, Canada, for earlier despatches.
T24.   10 rolls.

Despatches From U.S. Consuls in Woodstock, Canada, 1882–1906.
T707.   1 roll.

Despatches From U.S. Consuls in Yarmouth, Canada, 1886–1906.
T708   3 rolls.

Despatches From U.S. Consuls in Yokohama, Japan, 1897–1906.
M136.   5 rolls.

Despatches From U.S. Consuls in Zacatecas, Mexico, 1860–1884.
See also Mexico City, Mexico.
M307.   1 roll.   DP.

Despatches From U.S. Consuls in Zante, Greece, 1853–1862.
T451.   3 rolls.

Despatches From U.S. Consuls in Zanzibar, British Africa, 1836–1906.
M468.   5 rolls.   DP.

Despatches From U.S. Consuls in Zittau, Germany, 1897–1906.
T709.   1 roll.

Despatches From U.S. Consuls in Zurich, Switzerland, 1852–1906.
T452.   8 rolls.

Notes From Foreign Legations

Notes From the Argentine Legation in the United States to the Department of State, 1811–1906.
M47.   14 rolls.

Notes From the Austrian Legation in the United States to the Department of State, 1820–1906.
M48.   15 rolls.

Notes From the Belgian Legation in the United States to the Department of State, 1832–1906.
M194.   12 rolls.

Notes From the Bolivian Legation in the United States to the Department of State, 1837–1906.
T795.   1 roll.

Notes From the Brazilian Legation in the United States to the Department of State, 1824–1906.
M49.   8 rolls.   DP.

Notes From the British Legation in the United States to the Department of State, 1791–1906.
M50.   145 rolls.

Notes From Central American Legations in the United States to the Department of State, 1823–1906.
T34.   10 rolls.

Notes From the Chilean Legation in the United States to the Department of State, 1811–1906.
M73.   6 rolls.

Notes From the Chinese Legation in the United States to the Department of State, 1868–1906.
M98.   6 rolls.   DP.

Notes From the Colombian Legation in the United States to the Department of State, 1810–1906.
M51.   11 rolls.

Notes From the Costa Rican Legation in the United States to the Department of State, 1878–1906.
T799.   2 rolls.

Notes From the Cuban Legation in the United States to the Department of State, 1844–1906.
T800.   2 rolls.

Notes From the Danish Legation in the United States to the Department of State, 1801–1906.
M52.   9 rolls.

Notes From the Legation of the Dominican Republic in the United States to the Department of State, 1844–1906.
T801.   3 rolls.

Notes From the Ecuadorean Legation in the United States to the Department of State, 1839–1906.
T810.   2 rolls.

Notes From the Legation of El Salvador in the United States to the Department of State, 1879–1906.
T798.   2 rolls.

Notes From the French Legation in the United States to the Department of State, 1789–1906.
M53.   32 rolls.   DP.

Notes From the Legations of the German States and Germany in the United States to the Department of State, 1817–1906.
M58.   35 rolls.

Notes From the Greek Legation in the United States to the Department of State, 1823–1892.
T808.   1 roll.

Notes From the Haitian Legation in the United States to the Department of State, 1861–1906.
T803.   6 rolls.

Notes From the Hawaiian Legation in the United States to the Department of State, 1841–1899.
T160.   4 rolls.

Notes From the Honduran Legation in the United States to the Department of State, 1878–1906.
T796.   1 roll.

Notes From the Italian Legation in the United States to the Department of State, 1861–1906.
M202.   18 rolls.   DP.

Notes From the Japanese Legation in the United States to the Department of State, 1858–1906.
M163.   9 rolls.   DP.

Notes From the Korean Legation in the United States to the Department of State, 1883–1906.
M166.   1 roll.

Notes From the Liberian Legation in the United States to the Department of State, 1862–1898.
T807.   1 roll.

Notes From the Luxembourg Legation in the United States to the Department of State, 1876–1903.
T814.   1 roll.

Notes From the Madagascan Legation in the United States to the Department of State, 1883–1894.
T806.   1 roll.

Notes From the Mexican Legation in the United States to the Department of State, 1821–1906.
M54.   39 rolls.   DP.

Notes From Miscellaneous Foreign States to the Department of State, 1817–1906.
T953.   4 rolls.

Notes From the Montenegrin Legation in the United States to the Department of State, 1896–1905.
T614.   1 roll.

Notes From the Netherlands Legation in the United States to the Department of State, 1784–1906.
M56.   13 rolls.   DP.

Notes From the Nicaraguan Legation in the United States to the Department of State, 1862–1906.
T797.   4 rolls.

Notes From the Norwegian Legation in the United States to the Department of State, 1905–1906.
T811.   1 roll.

Notes From the Panamanian Legation in the United States to the Department of State, 1903–1906.
T812.   1 roll.

Notes From the Paraguayan Legation in the United States to the Department of State, 1853–1906.
M350.   1 roll.

Notes From the Persian Legation in the United States to the Department of State, 1887–1906.
M511.   1 roll.

Notes From the Peruvian Legation in the United States to the Department of State, 1827–1906.
T802.   6 rolls.

Notes From the Portuguese Legation in the United States to the Department of State, 1796–1906.
M57.   8 rolls.

Notes From the Russian Legation in the United States to the Department of State, 1809–1906.
M39.   12 rolls. DP.

Notes From the Samoan Legation in the United States to the Department of State, 1856–1894.
T805.   1 roll.

Notes From the Sardinian Legation in the United States to the Department of State, 1838–1861.
M201.   1 roll.

Notes From the Siamese Legation in the United States to the Department of State, 1876–1906.
M512.   1 roll.   DP.

Notes From the Kingdom of the Two Sicilies Legation in the United States to the Department of State, 1826–1860.
M55.   2 rolls.

Notes From the Spanish Legation in the United States to the Department of State, 1790–1906.
M59.   31 rolls. DP.

Notes From the Swedish Legation in the United States to the Department of State, 1813–1906.
M60.   9 rolls.

Notes From the Swiss Legation in the United States to the Department of State, 1882–1906.
T813.   6 rolls.

Notes From the Texan Legation in the United States to the Department of State, 1836–1845.
T809.   1 roll.

Notes From the Tunisian Legation in the United States to the Department of State, 1805–1806.
M67.   1 roll.

Notes From the Turkish Legation in the United States to the Department of State, 1867–1906.
T815.   8 rolls.

Notes From the Uruguayan Legation in the United States to the Department of State, 1834–1906.
T804.   1 roll.

Notes From the Venezuelan Legation in the United States to the Department of State, 1835–1906.
T93.   8 rolls.

Notes To and From Foreign Legations and Consulates

Notes From the Department of State to Foreign Ministers and Consuls in the United States, 1793–1834.
M38.   5 rolls.

Notes to Foreign Legations in the United States From the Department of State, 1834–1906.
M99.   99 rolls.

Notes to Foreign Consuls in the United States From the Department of State, 1853–1906.
M663.   4 rolls.

Notes From Foreign Consuls in the United States to the Department of State, 1789–1906.
M664.   11 rolls.

Decimal File, 1910–1963

Manual for Classification of Correspondence, Department of State (4th ed., 1938).
M600.   1 roll.

Purport Lists for the Department of State Decimal File, 1910–1944.
M973.   654 rolls. DP.

Records of the Department of State, Records Codification Manual, Central Decimal File, 1950–1963.
M1275.   1 roll.

Records of the Department of State Relating to Internal Affairs of Afghanistan, 1930–1944.
M1219.   7 rolls.

Records of the Department of State Relating to the Internal Affairs of Albania, 1910–1944.
M1211.   16 rolls.

Records of the Department of State Relating to Political Relations Between the United States and Other American States (Monroe Doctrine), 1910–1949.
M1276.   30 rolls.

Records of the Department of State Relating to Internal Affairs of Argentina, 1910–1929.
M514.   44 rolls. DP.

Records of the Department of State Relating to Internal Affairs of Argentina, 1930–1939.
M1230.   32 rolls.

Records of the Department of State Relating to Internal Affairs of Argentina, 1940–1944.
M1322.   40 rolls.

Records of the Department of State Relating to Political Relations Between the United States and Argentina, 1910–1929.
M515.   1 roll.   DP.

Records of the Department of State Relating to Political Relations Between Argentina and Other States, 1910–1929.
M516.   1 roll.   DP.

Records of the Department of State Relating to Internal Affairs of Armenia, 1910–1929.
T1192.   8 rolls.

Records of the Department of State Relating to Political Relations Between Armenia and Other States, 1910–1929.
T1193.   2 rolls.

Records of the Department of State Relating to Internal Affairs of Asia, 1910–1929.
M722.   28 rolls. DP.

Records of the Department of State Relating to Political Relations Between the United States and Asia, 1920–1929.
M723.   1 roll.   DP.

Records of the Department of State Relating to Political Relations Between Asia and Other States, 1910–1929.
M724.   1 roll.   DP.

Records of the Department of State Relating to Internal Affairs of Austria-Hungary and Austria, 1910–1929.
M695.   69 rolls. DP.

Records of the Department of State Relating to Political Relations Between the United States and Austria-Hungary and Austria, 1910–1929.
M696.   4 rolls.   DP.

Records of the Department of State Relating to Political Relations Between Austria-Hungary and Austria and Other States, 1910–1929.
M697.   3 rolls.   DP.

Records of the Department of
State Relating to Internal Affairs of
Austria-Hungary and Hungary,
1912–1929.
M708.   38 rolls.   DP.

Records of the Department of State
Relating to Political Relations Between
the United States and Austria-Hungary
and Hungary, 1921–1929.
M709.   1 roll.   DP.

Records of the Department of State
Relating to Political Relations Between
Austria-Hungary and Hungary and
Other States, 1920–1929.
M710.   2 rolls.   DP.

Records of the Department of State
Relating to Internal Affairs of Austria,
1930–1944.
M1209.   32 rolls.

Records of the Department of State
Relating to Internal Affairs of
Australia, 1910–1944.
T1190.   36 rolls.

Records of the Department of State
Relating to Political Relations
Between the United States and
Australia, 1910–1944.
T1191.   1 roll.

Records of the Department of State
Relating to Internal Affairs of the
Balkan States, 1910–1939.
M1447.   5 rolls.

Records of the Department of State
Relating to Internal Affairs of the
Balkan States, 1940–1944.
M1220.   1 roll.

Records of the Department of State
Relating to Internal Affairs of the
Baltic States, 1910–1944.
M1185.   8 rolls.

Records of the Department of State
Relating to Internal Affairs of Belgium,
1910–1929.
M675.   78 rolls.   DP.

Records of the Department of State
Relating to Political Relations
Between the United States and
Belgium, 1910–1929.
M676.   1 roll.   DP.

Records of the Department of State
Relating to Political Relations
Between Belgium and Other States,
1910–1929.
M677.   4 rolls.   DP.

Records of the Department of State
Relating to Internal Affairs of Bolivia,
1910–1929.
M644.   33 rolls.   DP.

Records of the Department of State
Relating to Political Relations
Between Bolivia and Other
States, 1910–1929.
M646.   18 rolls.   DP.

Records of the Department of State
Relating to Internal Affairs of Brazil,
1910–1929.
M519.   54 rolls.   DP.

Records of the Department of State
Relating to Internal Affairs of Brazil,
1930–1939.
M1472.   48 rolls.

Records of the Department of State
Relating to Internal Affairs of Brazil,
1940–1944.
M1515.   84 rolls.

Records of the Department of State
Relating to Internal Affairs of Brazil,
1945–1949.
M1492.   48 rolls.   DP.

Records of the Department of State
Relating to Internal Political and
National Defense Affairs of Brazil,
1950–1954.
M1487.   14 rolls.   DP.

Records of the Department of State
Relating to Internal Economic,
Industrial, and Social Affairs of Brazil,
1950–1954.
M1489.   34 rolls.   DP.

Records of the Department of State
Relating to Political Relations
Between the United States and Brazil,
1910–1929.
M525.   1 roll.   DP.

Records of the Department of
State Relating to Political Relations
Between Brazil and Other States,
1910–1929.
M526.   2 rolls.   DP.

Records of the Department of State
Relating to Internal Political and
National Defense Affairs of Brazil,
1955–59.
M1511.   8 rolls.

Records of the Department of State
Relating to Internal Affairs of British
Africa, 1910–1929.
M583.   33 rolls.   DP.

Records of the Department of State
Relating to Political Relations Between
the United States and British Africa,
1910–1929.
M584.   1 roll.

Records of the Department of State
Relating to Political Relations Between
British Africa and Other States, 1910–
1929.
M585.   1 roll.

Records of the Department of State
Relating to Internal Affairs of British
Asia, 1910–1929.
M712.   21 rolls.   DP.

Records of the Department of State
Relating to Political Relations Between
British Asia and Other States, Including
the United States, 1910–1929.
M713.   1 roll.   DP.

Records of the Department of State
Relating to Internal Affairs of Bulgaria,
1910–1944.
M1207.   21 rolls.

Records of the Department of State
Relating to Internal Affairs of Canada,
1910–1929.
M1435.   54 rolls.

Records of the Department of State
Relating to Internal Affairs of Central
America, 1910–1929.
M672.   16 rolls.   DP.

Records of the Department of State
Relating to Internal Affairs of Central
America, 1930–1949.
M1330.   6 rolls.

Records of the Department of State
Relating to Political Relations Between
the United States and Central America,
1911–1929.
M673.   1 roll.   DP.

Records of the Department of State
Relating to Political Relations Between
Central America and Other States,
1910–1929.
M674.   2 rolls.   DP.

Records of the Department of State
Relating to Internal Affairs of Chile,
1910–1929.
M487.   40 rolls.   DP.

Records of the Department of State
Relating to Political Relations Between
the United States and Chile,
1910–1929.
M489.   1 roll.   DP.

Records of the Department of
State Relating to Political Relations
Between Chile and Other States,
1910–1929.
M490.   2 rolls.   DP.

Records of the Department of State
Relating to Internal Affairs of China,
1910–1929.
M329.   227 rolls. DP.

Records of the Department of
State Relating to Political Relations
Between the United States and China,
1910–1929.
M339.   2 rolls.   DP.

Records of the Department of
State Relating to Political Relations
Between China and Japan,
1930–1944.
M976.   96 rolls. DP.

Records of the Department of
State Relating to Political Relations
Between China and Other States,
1910–1929.
M341.   34 rolls. DP.

Records of the Department of State
Relating to Internal Affairs of
Colombia, 1910–1929.
M1294. 45 rolls.

Records of the Department of State
Relating to Internal Affairs of Costa
Rica, 1910–1929.
M669.   40 rolls. DP.

Records of the Department of State
Relating to Political Relations Between
the United States and Costa Rica,
1910–1929.
M670.   1 roll.   DP.

Records of the Department of
State Relating to Political Relations
Between Costa Rica and Other States,
1910–1929.
M671.   10 rolls. DP.

Records of the Department of State
Relating to Internal Affairs of Cuba,
1910–1929.
M488.   99 rolls. DP.

Records of the Department of
State Relating to Political Relations
Between the United States and Cuba,
1910–1929.
M509.   2 rolls.   DP.

Records of the Department of State
Relating to Political Relations Between
Cuba and Other States, 1910–1929.
M510.   1 roll.   DP.

Records of the Department of State
Relating to Internal Affairs of
Czechoslovakia, 1910–1944.
M1218. 32 rolls.

Records of the Department Relating to
Internal Affairs of the Free City of
Danzig, 1910–1929.
M1378. 11 rolls.

Records of the Department of State
Relating to Internal Affairs of
Denmark, 1910–1939.
M1452. 38 rolls.

Records of the Department of
State Relating to Internal Affairs
of the Dominican Republic,
1910–1929.
M626.   79 rolls.

Records of the Department of State
Relating to Internal Affairs of the
Dominican Republic, 1930–1939.
M1272. 37 rolls.

Records of the Department of State
Relating to Internal Affairs of the
Dominican Republic, 1940–1944.
M1277. 20 rolls.

Records of the Department of State
Relating to Political Relations of
Eastern Europe, 1930–1939.
T1243. 46 rolls.

Records of the Department of State
Relating to Political Relations of
Eastern Europe, 1940–1944.
T1244. 5 rolls.

Records of the Department of State
Relating to Internal Affairs of Ecuador,
1910–1929.
M1468. 27 rolls.

Records of the Department of State
Relating to Internal Affairs of Egypt,
1910–1929.
M571.   31 rolls. DP.

Records of the Department of State
Relating to Internal Affairs of Egypt,
1930–1939.
T1251. 22 rolls.

Records of the Department of
State Relating to Political Relations
Between the United States and
Egypt, 1910–1929.
M572.   1 roll.   DP.

Records of the Department of State
Relating to Political Relations Between
Egypt and Other States, 1910–1929.
M573.   1 roll.   DP.

Records of the Department of State
Relating to Internal Affairs of
El Salvador, 1910–1929.
M658.   22 rolls. DP.

Records of the Department of
State Relating to Political Relations
Between the United States and El
Salvador, 1910–1929.
M659.   1 roll.   DP.

Records of the Department of
State Relating to Political Relations
Between El Salvador and Other
States, 1910–1929.
M660.   1 roll.   DP.

Records of the Department of State
Relating to Internal Affairs of Estonia,
1910–1944.
M1170. 23 rolls.

Records of the Department of State
Relating to Internal Affairs of Ethiopia,
1910–1929.
M411.   4 rolls.   DP.

Records of the Department of
State Relating to Political Relations
Between the United States and
Ethiopia, 1910–1929.
M412   1 roll.   DP.

Records of the Department of State
Relating to Internal Affairs of Finland,
1910–1944.
T1184. 32 rolls.

Records of the Department of
State Relating to Political Relations
Between the United States and
Finland, 1910–1944.
T1185. 2 rolls.

Records of the Department of
State Relating to Political Relations
Between Finland and Other States,
1910–1944.
T1186. 8 rolls.

Records of the Department of State
Relating to Internal Affairs of France,
1910–1929.
M560.   162 rolls. DP.

Records of the Department of State
Relating to Internal Affairs of France,
1930–1939.
M1442. 89 rolls.

Records of the Department of
State Relating to Political Relations
Between the United States and
France, 1910–1929.
M563.   5 rolls.   DP.

Records of the Department of State Relating to Political Relations Between France and Other States, 1910–1929.
M569. 7 rolls. DP.

Records of the Department of State Relating to Internal Affairs of Germany, 1910–1929.
M336. 182 rolls. DP.

Records of the Department of State Relating to Political Relations Between the United States and Germany, 1910–1929.
M355. 4 rolls. DP.

Records of the Department of State Relating to Political Relations Between the United States and Germany, 1930–1939.
T1253. 2 rolls.

Records of the Department of State Relating to Political Relations Between Germany and Other States, 1910–1929.
M354. 4 rolls. DP.

Records of the Department of State Relating to Internal Affairs of Great Britain, 1910–1929.
M580. 249 rolls. DP.

Records of the Department of State Relating to Internal Affairs of Great Britain, 1930–1939.
M1455. 78 rolls.

Records of the Department of State Relating to Political Relations Between the United States and Great Britain, 1910–1929.
M581. 15 rolls. DP.

Records of the Department of State Relating to Political Relations Between the United States and Great Britain, 1930–1939.
T1252. 6 rolls.

Records of the Department of State Relating to Political Relations Between Great Britain and Other States, 1910–1929.
M582. 13 rolls. DP.

Records of the Department of State Relating to Internal Affairs of Greece, 1910–1929.
M443. 45 rolls. DP.

Records of the Department of State Relating to Internal Affairs of Greece, 1930–1939.
M1179. 16 rolls.

Records of the Department of State Relating to Political Relations Between the United States and Greece, 1910–1929.
M475. 3 rolls.

Records of the Department of State Relating to Political Relations Between Greece and Other States, 1910–1929.
M476. 6 rolls. DP.

Records of the Department of State Relating to Internal Affairs of Guatemala, 1910–1929.
M655. 40 rolls. DP.

Records of the Department of State Relating to Internal Affairs of Guatemala, 1930–1944.
M1280. 22 rolls.

Records of the Department of State Relating to Internal Affairs of Guatemala, 1945–1949.
M1527. 12 rolls.

Records of the Department of State Relating to Political Relations Between the United States and Guatemala, 1910–1929.
M656. 1 roll. DP.

Records of the Department of State Relating to Political Relations Between Guatemala and Other States, 1910–1929.
M657. 27 rolls. DP.

Records of the Department of State Relating to Internal Affairs of Haiti, 1910–1929.
M610. 94 rolls. DP.

Records of the Department of State Relating to Internal Affairs of Haiti, 1930–1939.
M1246. 36 rolls.

Records of the Department of State Relating to Political Relations Between the United States and Haiti, 1910–1929.
M611. 2 rolls.

Records of the Department of State Relating to Political Relations Between Haiti and Other States, 1910–1929.
M612. 4 rolls.

Records of the Department of State Relating to Internal Affairs of Honduras, 1910–1929.
M647. 49 rolls. DP.

Records of the Department of State Relating to Political Relations Between the United States and Honduras, 1910–1929.
M648. 1 roll. DP.

Records of the Department of State Relating to Internal Affairs of Hungary, 1930–1944.
M1206. 17 rolls.

Records of the Department of State Relating to Internal Affairs of India and Burma, 1910–1929.
M335. 26 rolls. DP.

Records of the Department of State Relating to Political Relations Between the United States and India and Burma, 1910–1929.
M343. 1 roll.

Records of the Department of State Relating to Political Relations Between India and Burma and Other States, 1910–1929.
M344. 1 roll.

Records of the Department of State Relating to Internal Affairs of Iran, 1930–1939.
M1202. 24 rolls.

Records of the Department of State Relating to Internal Affairs of Iraq, 1930–1944.
T1180. 18 rolls.

➤Records of the Department of State Relating to Internal Affairs of the Republic of Ireland and Northern Ireland.
M1231. 17 rolls.

Records of the Department of State Relating to Internal Affairs of Italy, 1910–1929.
M527. 60 rolls. DP.

Records of the Department of State Relating to Internal Affairs of Italy, 1930–1939.
M1423. 33 rolls.

Records of the Department of State Relating to Political Relations Between the United States and Italy, 1910–1929.
M529. 3 rolls. DP.

Records of the Department of State Relating to Political Relations Between Italy and Other States, 1910–1929.
M530. 8 rolls. DP.

Records of the Department of State Relating to Internal Affairs of Japan, 1910–1929.
M422.   43 rolls.   DP.

Records of the Department of State Relating to Political Relations Between the United States and Japan, 1910–1929.
M423.   9 rolls.   DP.

Records of the Department of State Relating to Political Relations Between Japan and Other States, 1910–1929.
M424.   1 roll.   DP.

Records of the Department of State Relating to Internal Affairs of Korea, 1910–1929.
M426.   9 rolls.   DP.

Records of the Department of State Relating to Internal Affairs of Latvia, 1910–1944.
M1177.   19 rolls.

Records of the Department of State Relating to Internal Affairs of Lebanon, 1930–1944.
T1178.   5 rolls.

Records of the Department of State Relating to Internal Affairs of Liberia, 1910–1929.
M613.   34 rolls.   DP.

Records of the Department of State Relating to Political Relations Between Liberia and Other States, Including the United States, 1919–1929.
M614.   1 roll.   DP.

Records of the Department of State Relating to Internal Affairs of Lithuania, 1910–1944.
M1178.   22 rolls.

Records of the Department of State Relating to Internal Affairs of Mexico, 1910–1929.
M274.   243 rolls. DP.

Records of the Department of State Relating to Internal Affairs of Mexico, 1930–1939.
M1370.   165 rolls.

Records of the Department of State Relating to Political Relations Between the United States and Mexico, 1910–1929.
M314.   29 rolls.   DP.

Records of the Department of State Relating to Political Relations Between Mexico and Other States, 1910–1929.
M315.   2 rolls.   DP.

Records of the Department of State Relating to Internal Affairs of Montenegro and to Political Relations Between the United States and Montenegro, 1910–1929.
M349.   2 rolls

Records of the Department of State Relating to Internal Affairs of Morocco, 1910–1929.
M577.   26 rolls.   DP.

Records of the Department of State Relating to Political Relations Between the United States and Morocco, 1910–1929.
M578.   1 roll.   DP.

Records of the Department of State Relating to Political Relations Between Morocco and Other States, 1910–1929.
M579.   1 roll.   DP.

Records of the Department of State Relating to Internal Affairs of The Netherlands, 1910–1929.
M682.   54 rolls. DP.

Records of the Department of State Relating to Political Relations Between the United States and The Netherlands, 1910–1929.
M683.   6 rolls.   DP.

Records of the Department of State Relating to Political Relations Between The Netherlands and Other States, 1910–1929.
M684.   1 roll.   DP.

Records of the Department of State Relating to Internal Affairs of Nicaragua, 1910–1929.
M632.   106 rolls. DP.

Records of the Department of State Relating to Internal Affairs of Nicaragua, 1930–1944.
M1273.   53 rolls.

Records of the Department of State Relating to Political Relations Between the United States and Nicaragua, 1910–1929.
M633.   2 rolls.

Records of the Department of State Relating to Political Relations Between Nicaragua and Other States, 1910–1929.
M634.   3 rolls.

Records of the Department of State Relating to Internal Affairs of Norway, 1910–1939.
M1406.   22 rolls.

Records of the Department of State Relating to Internal Affairs of Pakistan, 1945–1949.
M1448.   6 rolls.

Records of the Department of State Relating to Internal Affairs of Palestine, 1930–1944.
M1037.   26 rolls.   DP.

Records of the Department of State Relating to Internal Affairs of Palestine, 1945–1949.
M1390.   27 rolls.

Records of the Department of State Relating to Internal Affairs of Panama, 1910–1929.
M607.   58 rolls.   DP.

Records of the Department of State Relating to Political Relations Between the United States and Panama, 1910–1929.
M608   14 rolls.

Records of the Department of State Relating to Political Relations Between Panama and Other States, 1910–1929.
M609.   3 rolls.   DP.

Records of the Department of State Relating to Internal Affairs of the Papal States (Holy See), 1910–1929.
M561.   1 roll.

Records of the Department of State Relating to Political Relations Between the United States and the Papal States (Holy See), 1910–1929.
M562.   1 roll.

Records of the Department of State Relating to Political Relations Between the Papal States (Holy See) and Other States, 1910–1929.
M563.   1 roll.

Records of the Department of State Relating to Internal Affairs of Paraguay, 1910–1939.
M1470.   22 rolls.

Records of the Department of State Relating to Internal Affairs of Persia, 1910–1929.
M715.   37 rolls.   DP.

Records of the Department of State Relating to Political Relations Between the United States and Persia, 1921–1929.
M716.   1 roll.   DP.

Records of the Department of State Relating to Political Relations Between Persia and Other States, 1921–1929.
M717.   1 roll.   DP.

Records of the Department of State Relating to Internal Affairs of Peru, 1910–1929.
M746.   30 rolls.   DP.

Records of the Department of State Relating to Political Relations Between Peru and Other States, 1910–1929.
M748.   52 rolls.   DP.

Records of the Department of State Relating to Internal Affairs of Poland, 1916–1944.
M1197.   75 rolls.

Records of the Department of State Relating to Internal Affairs of Portugal, 1910–1929.
M705.   34 rolls.   DP.

Records of the Department of State Relating to Internal Affairs of Romania, 1910–1944.
M1198.   44 rolls.

Records of the Department of State Relating to Internal Affairs of Russia and the Soviet Union, 1910–1929.
M316.   177 rolls. DP.

Records of the Department of State Relating to Internal Affairs of the Soviet Union, 1930–1939.
T1249.   75 rolls.

Records of the Department of State Relating to Internal Affairs of the Soviet Union, 1940–1944.
T1250.   34 rolls.

Records of the Department of State Relating to Political Relations Between the United States and Russia and the Soviet Union, 1910–1929.
M333.   7 rolls.   DP.

Records of the Department of State Relating to Political Relations Between the United States and the Soviet Union, 1930–1939.
T1241.   3 rolls.

Records of the Department of State Relating to Political Relations Between the United States and the Soviet Union, 1940–1944.
T1242.   1 roll.

Records of the Department of State Relating to Political Relations Between Russia and the Soviet Union and Other States, 1910–1929.
M340.   20 rolls.   DP.

Records of the Department of State Relating to Political Relations Between the Soviet Union and Other States, 1930–1939.
T1247.   14 rolls.

Records of the Department of State Relating to Political Relations Between the Soviet Union and Other States, 1940–1944.
T1248.   4 rolls.

Records of the Department of State Relating to Internal Affairs of Saudi Arabia, 1930–1944.
T1179.   8 rolls.

Records of the Department of State Relating to Internal Affairs of Serbia and to Political Relations Between the United States and Serbia, 1910–1929.
M357.   3 rolls.

Records of the Department of State Relating to Internal Affairs of Siam, 1910–1929.
M729.   18 rolls.   DP.

Records of the Department of State Relating to Political Relations Between the United States and Siam, 1910–1929.
M730.   1 roll.   DP.

Records of the Department of State Relating to Political Relations Between Siam and Other States, 1910–1929.
M731.   1 roll.   DP.6.

Records of the Department of State Relating to Internal Affairs of Spain, 1910–1929.
M1369.   38 rolls.

Records of the Department of State Relating to Internal Affairs of Sweden, 1910–1939.
M1424.   44 rolls.

Records of the Department of State Relating to Internal Affairs of Switzerland, 1910–1939.
M1457.   27 rolls.

Records of the Department of State Relating to Internal Affairs of Syria, 1930–1944.
T1177.   11 rolls.

Records of the Department of State Relating to Internal Affairs of Trans-Jordan, 1930–1944.
T1181.   1 roll.

Records of the Department of State Relating to Internal Affairs of Turkey, 1910–1929.
M353.   88 rolls.   DP.

Records of the Department of State Relating to Internal Affairs of Turkey, 1930–1944.
M1224.   36 rolls.

Records of the Department of State Relating to Internal Affairs of Turkey, 1945–1949.
M1292.   20 rolls.

Records of the Department of State Relating to Political Relations Between the United States and Turkey, 1910–1929.
M365.   8 rolls.   DP.

Records of the Department of State Relating to Political Relations Between the United States and Turkey, 1930–1944.
M1223.   2 rolls.

Records of the Department of State Relating to Political Relations Between Turkey and Other States, 1910–1929.
M363.   29 rolls.   DP.

Records of the Department of State Relating to Political Relations of Turkey, Greece, and the Balkan States, 1930–1939.
T1245.   11 rolls.

Records of the Department of State Relating to Political Relations of Turkey, Greece, and the Balkan States, 1940–1944.
T1246.   2 rolls.

Records of the Department of State Relating to Internal Affairs of Venezuela, 1910–1929.
M366.   32 rolls.   DP.

Records of the Department of State Relating to Political Relations Between the United States and Venezuela, 1910–1929.
M368.   1 roll.   DP.

Records of the Department of State Relating to Political Relations Between Venezuela and Other States, 1910–1929.
M369.   2 rolls.

Records of the Department of State Relating to Internal Affairs of Yugoslavia, 1910–1929.
M358.   27 rolls.   DP.

Records of the Department of State Relating to Internal Affairs of Yugoslavia, 1930–1944.
M1203.   28 rolls.

Records of the Department of State Relating to Political Relations Between the United States and Yugoslavia, 1910–1929.
M362.   1 roll.   DP.

Records of the Department of State Relating to Political Relations Between Yugoslavia and Other States, 1910–1929.
M361.   9 rolls.   DP.

State Department Territorial Papers

State Department Territorial Papers, Arizona, 1864–1872.
M342.   1 roll.   DP.

State Department Territorial Papers, Colorado, 1859–1874.
M3.   1 roll.   DP.

State Department Territorial Papers, Dakota, 1861–1873.
M309.   1 roll.   DP.

State Department Territorial Papers, Florida, 1777–1824.
M116.   11 rolls.

State Department Territorial Papers, Idaho, 1863–1872.
M445.   1 roll.   DP.

State Department Territorial Papers, Kansas, 1854–1861.
M218.   2 rolls.   DP.

State Department Territorial Papers, Missouri, 1812–1820.
M1134.   1 roll.

State Department Territorial Papers, Montana, 1864–1872.
M356.   2 rolls.   DP.

State Department Territorial Papers, Nebraska, 1854–1867.
M228.   1 roll.   DP.

State Department Territorial Papers, Nevada, 1861–1864.
M13.   2 rolls.

State Department Territorial Papers, New Mexico, 1851–1872.
T17.   4 rolls.

State Department Territorial Papers, Oregon, 1848–1858.
M419.   1 roll.

State Department Territorial Papers, Orleans, 1764–1813.
T260.   13 rolls.

State Department Territorial Papers, Territory Northwest of the River Ohio, 1787–1801.
M470.   1 roll.   DP.

State Department Territorial Papers, Territory Southwest of the River Ohio, 1790–1795.
M471.   1 roll.   DP.

State Department Territorial Papers, Utah, 1853–1873.
M12.   2 rolls.   DP.

State Department Territorial Papers, Washington, 1854–1872.
M26.   2 rolls.

State Department Territorial Papers, Wyoming, 1868–1873.
M85.   1 roll.

Letters of Application and Recommendation

Letters of Application and Recommendation During the Administration of John Adams, 1797–1801.
M406.   3 rolls.   DP.

Letters of Application and Recommendation During the Administration of Thomas Jefferson, 1801–1809.
M418.   12 rolls.   DP.

Letters of Application and Recommendation During the Administration of James Madison, 1809–1817.
M438.   8 rolls.   DP.

Letters of Application and Recommendation During the Administration of James Monroe, 1817–1825.
M439.   19 rolls.   DP.

Letters of Application and Recommendation During the Administration of John Quincy Adams, 1825–1829.
M531.   8 rolls.   DP.

Letters of Application and Recommendation During the Administration of Andrew Jackson, 1829–1837.
M639.   27 rolls.   DP.

Letters of Application and Recommendation During the Administrations of Martin Van Buren, William Henry Harrison, and John Tyler, 1837–1845.
M687.   35 rolls.   DP.

Letters of Application and Recommendation During the Administrations of James Polk, Zachary Taylor, and Millard Fillmore, 1845–1853.
M873.   98 rolls.   DP.

Letters of Application and Recommendation During the Administrations of Franklin Pierce and James Buchanan, 1853–1861.
M967.   50 rolls.   DP.

Letters of Application and Recommendation During the Administrations of Abraham Lincoln and Andrew Johnson, 1861–1869.
M650.   52 rolls.   DP.

Letters of Application and Recommendation During the Administration of Ulysses S. Grant, 1869–1877.
M968.   69 rolls.   DP.

Other General Records of the Department of State

Registers of Correspondence of the Department of State, 1870–1906.
M17.   71 rolls.

Records of Negotiations Connected With the Treaty of Ghent, 1813–1815.
M36.   2 rolls.

Despatches From Special Agents of the Department of State, 1794–1906.
M37.   22 rolls.   DP.

Domestic Letters of the Department of State, 1784–1906.
M40.   171 rolls.

Journal of the Voyage of the U.S.S. *Nonsuch* up the Orinoco, July 11–August 24, 1819.
M83.   1 roll.

Journal of Charles Mason, Kept During the Survey of the Mason and Dixon Line, 1763–1768.
M86. 1 roll. DP.

Miscellaneous Letters of the Department of State, 1789–1906.
M179. 1,310 rolls. DP.

Consular Trade Reports, 1943–1950.
M238. 681 rolls. 16mm.

Records of the Department of State Relating to World War I and Its Termination, 1914–1929.
M367. 518 rolls. DP.

Copybooks of George Washington's Correspondence With Secretaries of State, 1789–1796.
M570. 1 roll. DP.

List of U.S. Diplomatic Officers, 1789–1939.
M586. 3 rolls. DP.

List of U.S. Consular Officers, 1789–1939.
M587. 21 rolls. DP.

"War of 1812 Papers" of the Department of State, 1789–1815.
M588. 7 rolls. DP.

Records of the Department of State Special Interrogation Mission to Germany, 1945–1946.
M679. 3 rolls.

Personal and Confidential Letters From Secretary of State Lansing to President Wilson, 1915–1918.
M743. 1 roll. DP.

Reports of Clerks and Bureau Officers of the Department of State, 1790–1911.
M800. 8 rolls. DP.

Numerical and Minor Files of the Department of State, 1906–1910.
M862. 1,241 rolls. DP.

Records of the Department of State Relating to Guano Islands, 1852–1912.
M974. 7 rolls. DP.

Records of the Department of State Relating to World War II, 1939–1945.
M982. 252 rolls. DP.

Marshall/Lovett Memorandums to President Truman, 1947–1948.
M1135. 3 rolls. DP.

Policy Planning Staff Numbered Papers, 1–63; 1947–1949.
M1171. 71 cards (microfiche).

Palestine Reference Files of Dean Rusk and Robert McClintock, 1947–1949.
M1175. 12 rolls. DP.

Intelligence Reports, 1941–1961.*
M1221. Approximately 9,000 cards (microfiche).
*These records continue to be filmed. Contact the Textual Reference Branch (NNR2) for information.

Records of the Office of European Affairs, 1934–1947.
M1244. 18 rolls. DP.

Records of the Department of State Relating to the Problems of Relief and Refugees in Europe Arising from World War II and Its Aftermath, 1938–1949.
M1284. 70 rolls. DP.

Registers and Indexes for Passport Applications, 1810–1906.
M1371. 13 rolls. DP.

➤Passport Applications, 1795–1905.
M1372. 694 rolls.

➤Records of the Polish Ministry of Foreign Affairs, 1918–1940.
M1751. 56 rolls.

Minutes of Treaty Conferences Between the United States and Japanese Representatives, and Treaty Drafts, 1872.
T119. 1 roll.

Correspondence Relating to the Filibustering Expedition Against the Spanish Government of Mexico, 1811–1816.
T286. 1 roll.

Records of the Department of State Relating to Property Claims of U.S. Citizens Against Poland, 1930–1944.
T461. 8 rolls.

Miscellaneous Documents Relating to Reciprocity Negotiations of the Department of State, 1848–1854, 1884–1885, 1891–1892.
T493. 1 roll.

Papers Relating to the Cession of Alaska, 1856–1867; Enclosures 2 and 3 to Despatch 2115, Dated Dec. 2, 1936, From the U.S. Embassy in the Soviet Union.
T495. 1 roll.

Records of the Department of State Relating to U.S. Claims Against Russia, 1910–1929.
T640. 8 rolls.

Acceptances and Orders for Commissions in the Records of the Department of State, 1789–1828.
T645. 2 rolls.

Resignations and Declinations Among the Records of the Department of State, 1789–1827.
T730. 1 roll.

Correspondence of Secretary of State Bryan With President Wilson, 1913–1915.
M1517. 4 rolls.

Daybook of the Department of State for Miscellaneous and Contingent Expenses, Feb. 1, 1798–Nov. 3, 1820.
T903. 1 roll.

Cashbook of the Department of State, 1785–1795.
T904. 1 roll.

Despatches Received by the Department of State From the U.S. Commission to Central and South America, July 14, 1884–December 26, 1885.
T908. 1 roll.

Copies of Presidential Pardons and Remissions, 1794–1893.
T967. 7 rolls.

The Alaska Treaty, by David Hunter Miller, Department of State.
T1024. 1 roll.

Codebooks of the Department of State, 1867–1876.
T1171. 1 roll.

Minutes of Meetings of the Interdivisional Area Committee on the Far East, 1943–1946.
T1197. 1 roll.

Records of Special Agents for Securing the Florida Archives, 1819–1835.
T1212. 6 rolls.

State Department Documents of the Interdivisional Country and Area Committee, 1943–1946.
T1221. 6 rolls.

State Department Documents of the Post War Programs Committee, 1944.
T1222. 4 rolls.

General Records of the Department of Justice. RG 60

Letters Sent by the Department of Justice: General and Miscellaneous, 1818–1904.
M699.   81 rolls.   DP.

Letters Sent by the Department of Justice Concerning Judiciary Expenses, 1849–1884.
M700.   24 rolls.   DP.

Letters Sent by the Department of Justice: Instructions to U.S. Attorneys and Marshals, 1867–1904.
M701.   212 rolls. DP.

Letters Sent by the Department of Justice to Executive Officers and Members of Congress, 1871–1904.
M702.   91 rolls.   DP.

Letters Sent by the Department of Justice to Judges and Clerks, 1874–1904.
M703.   34 rolls.   DP.0.

Letters Received by the Department of Justice From the State of Alabama, 1871–1884.
M1356.   7 rolls.   DP.

Letters Received by the Department of Justice From the State of Arkansas, 1871–1884.
M1418.   5 rolls.   DP.

Letters Received by the Department of Justice From the Territory of Dakota, 1871–1884.
M1535.   3 rolls.   DP.

Letters Received by the Department of Justice From the State of Florida, 1871–1884.
M1327.   2 rolls.   DP.

Letters Received by the Department of Justice From the State of Georgia, 1871–1884.
M996.   5 rolls.   DP.4.

Letters Received by the Department of Justice From the State of Kentucky, 1871–1884.
M1362.   2 rolls.   DP.

Letters Received by the Department of Justice From the State of Louisiana, 1871–1884.
M940.   6 rolls.   DP.6.

Letters Received by the Department of Justice From the State of Maryland, 1871–1884.
M1352.   2 rolls.   DP.

Letters Received by the Department of Justice From Mississippi, 1871–1884.
M970.   4 rolls.   DP.

Letters Received by the Department of Justice From the State of North Carolina, 1871–1884.
M1345.   3 rolls.   DP.

Letters Received by the Department of Justice From South Carolina, 1871–1884.
M947.   9 rolls.   DP.0.

Letters Received by the Department of Justice From the State of Tennessee, 1871–1884.
M1471.   4 rolls.   DP.

Letters Received by the Department of Justice From the State of Texas, 1871–1884.
M1449.   7 rolls.

Letters Received by the Department of Justice From the State of Virginia, 1871–1884.
M1250.   4 rolls.   DP.

Records Relating to the Appointment of Federal Judges, Attorneys, and Marshals for the Territory and State of Idaho, 1861–1899.
M681.   9 rolls.   DP.

Records Relating to the Appointment of Federal Judges, Attorneys, and Marshals for Oregon, 1853–1903.
M224.   3 rolls.   DP.

Records Relating to the Appointment of Federal Judges, Attorneys, and Marshals for the Territory and State of Utah, 1853–1901.
M680.   14 rolls.   DP.

Records Relating to the Appointment of Federal Judges and U.S. Marshals for the Territory and State of Washington, 1853–1902.
M198.   17 rolls.   DP.1.

"The Pumpkin Papers": Microfilm Evidence Used in *United States* v. *Alger Hiss*, 1948–1951.
M1491.   1 roll.

Letters From and Opinions of the Attorneys General, 1791–1811.
T326.   1 roll.

Opinions of the Attorney General, 1817–1832.
T412.   3 rolls.

Index to Names of U.S. Marshals, 1789–1960.
T577.   1 roll.   16mm.

Records of the War Industries Board. RG 61

Minutes of War Industries Board Meetings, 1917–1918.
M1073.   2 rolls.   DP.

Records of the Council of National Defense. RG 62

Minutes of the Meetings of the Council of National Defense, 1916–1921; the Advisory Commission of the Council of National Defense, 1916–1918; the Interdepartmental Advisory Committee, 1917; the Joint Weekly Conference, 1917–1918; and the Interdepartmental Defense Board, 1919–1920.
M1069.   1 roll.

Minutes of Meetings of the Committee on Women's Defense Work, May 2, 1917–Feb. 12, 1919, and Weekly and Monthly Reports of the Committee on Women's Defense Work, May 12, 1917–Oct. 15, 1918.
M1074.   1 roll.

Records of the National Archives and Records Administration. RG 64

Federal Register, 1936–1983.
M190.   432 rolls. DP.

Publications of the National Archives, 1935–1968.
M248.   24 rolls.   DP.

National Archives Procedures: A General Services Administration Handbook (1960).
M604.   1 roll.

Weekly Compilations of Presidential Documents, 1965–1969.
M339.   5 rolls.

Guide to Records of the Italian Armed Forces.
T94.   1 roll.

Guide to German Records Microfilmed at Alexandria.
T733.   9 rolls.

National Archives Disposal Registers.
T820.   3 rolls.

Finding Aids to National Archives Photographs Relating to the Third German Reich.
M1137.   73 cards (microfiche).

The Archives of the U.S. Government: A Documentary History, 1774–1934, Compiled by Percy Scott Flippin.
T1167.   5 rolls.

Guide to Captured German Documents (Maxwell Air Force Base, Alabama, Dec. 1952) and *Supplement* (National Archives, Washington, DC, 1959).
T1183.   1 roll.

Prologue: The Journal of the National Archives, 1969–1978.
T1195.   2 rolls.

Records of the Federal Bureau of Investigation. RG 65

Investigative Case Files of the Bureau of Investigation, 1908–1922.
M1085.   955 rolls. DP.

➤Index to Federal Bureau of Investigation Class 61—Treason or Misprision of Treason, 1921–1931.
M1531.   15 rolls.   DP.

Records of the Commission of Fine Arts. RG 66

Photographs of the Commission of Fine Arts, 1901–1950.
M1148   9 rolls.

Records of the Work Projects Administration. RG 69

Records of the Federal Writers' Project, Work Projects Administration, Relating to Louisiana, 1935–1943.
M1366.   3 rolls.   DP.

Selected Documents From the Louisiana Section of the Work Projects Administration General Correspondence File ("State Series"), 1935–1943.
M1367.   30 rolls.   DP.

Index to Reference Cards for Work Projects Administration Project Files, 1935–1937.
T935.   79 rolls.   16mm.

Index to Reference Cards for Work Projects Administration Project Files, 1938.
T936.   15 rolls.   16mm.

Index to Reference Cards for Work Projects Administration Project Files, 1939–1942.
T937.   19 rolls.   16mm.

Records of the Bureau of Yards and Docks. RG 71

Annual Reports of the Department of the Navy, 1822–1866.
M1099.   8 rolls.   DP.

Plans of Buildings and Machinery Erected in the Navy Yard, Boston, 1830–1840.
T1023.   1 roll.

Records of the Bureau of Indian Affairs. RG 75

Letter Book of the Creek Trading House, 1795–1816.
M4.   1 roll.   DP.

Letters Sent by the Secretary of War Relating to Indian Affairs, 1800–1824.
M15.   6 rolls.

Register of Letters Received by the Office of Indian Affairs, 1824–1880.
M18.   126 rolls. DP.

Letters Sent by the Office of Indian Affairs, 1824–1881.
M21.   166 rolls. DP.

Letters Sent by the Superintendent of Indian Trade, 1807–1823.
M16.   6 rolls.   DP.

Letters of Tench Coxe, Commissioner of the Revenue, Relating to the Procurement of Military, Naval, and Indian Supplies, 1794–1796.
M74.   1 roll.   DP.

Letter Book of the Arkansas Trading House, 1805–1810.
M142.   1 roll.   DP.

Records of the Cherokee Indian Agency in Tennessee, 1801–1835.
M208.   14 rolls. DP.

Letters Received by the Office of Indian Affairs, 1824–1881.
M234.   962 rolls. DP.

Letters Received by the Office of the Secretary of War Relating to Indian Affairs, 1800–1823.
M271.   4 rolls.

Report Books of the Office of Indian Affairs, 1838–1885.
M348.   53 rolls. DP.

Special Files of the Office of Indian Affairs, 1807–1904.
M574.   85 rolls. DP.

Indian Census Rolls, 1884–1940.
M595.   692 rolls. DP.

Records Relating to Enrollment of Eastern Cherokee by Guion Miller, 1908–1910.
M685.   12 rolls.   DP.

Records Relating to Investigations of the Fort Philip Kearney (or Fetterman) Massacre, 1866–1867.
M740.   1 roll.   DP.

Miscellaneous Letters Sent by the Pueblo Indian Agency, 1874–1891.
M941.   10 rolls. DP.

Superintendent's Annual Narrative and Statistical Reports From Field Jurisdictions of the Bureau of Indian Affairs, 1907–1938.
M1011.   174 rolls. DP.

Selected Letters Received by the Office of Indian Affairs Relating to the Cherokee of North Carolina, 1851–1905.
M1059.   7 rolls.   DP.

Procedural Issuances of the Bureau of Indian Affairs: Orders and Circulars, 1854–1960.
M1121.   17 rolls.

Enrollment Cards for the Five Civilized Tribes, 1898–1914.
M1186.   93 rolls.   DP.

Miscellaneous Letters Sent by the Agent at the Pine Ridge Indian Agency, 1876–1914.
M1229. 76 rolls. DP.

Letters Sent to the Office of Indian Affairs by the Pine Ridge Agency, 1875–1914.
M1282. 52 rolls. DP.

Applications for Enrollment of the Commission to the Five Civilized Tribes, 1898–1914.
M1301. 468 rolls.

Records Created by Bureau of Indian Affairs Field Agencies Having Jurisdiction Over the Pueblo Records, 1874–1900.
M1304. 32 rolls. DP.

Index to Letters Received by the Commission to the Five Civilized Tribes, 1897–1913.
M1314. 23 rolls.

Records of the Alaska Division of the Bureau of Indian Affairs Concerning Metlakatla, 1887–1933.
M1333. 14 rolls.

Records of the Creek Factory of the Office of Indian Trade of the Bureau of Indian Affairs, 1795–1821.
M1334. 13 rolls.0.

Applications for Enrollment and Allotment of Washington Indians, 1911–1919.
M1343. 6 rolls.

Records Concerning Applications for Adoption by the Quinaielt Indians, 1910–1919.
M1344. 5 rolls.

Selected Records of the Bureau of Indian Affairs Relating to the Enrollment of Indians on the Flathead Reservation, 1903–1908.
M1350. 3 rolls.

Bureau of Indian Affairs Records Created by the Santa Fe Indian School, 1890–1918.
M1473. 38 rolls.

►Applications from the Bureau of Indian Affairs, Muskogee Area Office, Relating to Enrollment in the Five Civilized Tribes Under the Act of 1896.
M1650. 54 rolls. DP.

Letters Received by the Superintendent of Indian Trade, 1806–1824.
T58. 1 roll.

Census of Creek Indians Taken by Parsons and Abbott in 1832.
T275. 1 roll.

Documents Relating to the Negotiation of Ratified and Unratified Treaties With Various Indian Tribes, 1801–1869.
T494. 10 rolls.

Census Roll of the Cherokee Indians East of the Mississippi and Index to the Roll, 1835.
T496. 1 roll.

Records of the Choctaw Trading House, 1803–1824.
T500. 6 rolls.

"Old Settler" Cherokee Census Roll, 1895, and Index to Payment Roll, 1896.
T985. 2 rolls.

Letterbook of the Natchitoches-Sulphur Fork Factory, 1809–1821.
T1029. 1 roll.

Records of the Superintendencies of Indian Affairs

Records of the Arizona Superintendency of Indian Affairs, 1863–1873.
M734. 8 rolls. DP.

Records of the Central Superintendency of Indian Affairs, 1813–1878.
M856. 108 rolls. DP.

Records of the Dakota Superintendency of Indian Affairs, 1861–1870, 1877–1878, and the Wyoming Superintendency, 1870.
M1016. 13 rolls. DP.

Records of the Idaho Superintendency of Indian Affairs, 1863–1870.
M832. 3 rolls. DP.

Records of the Michigan Superintendency of Indian Affairs, 1814–1851.
M1. 71 rolls. DP.

Records of the Minnesota Superintendency of Indian Affairs, 1849–1856.
M842. 9 rolls. DP.

Records of the Montana Superintendency of Indian Affairs, 1867–1873.
M833. 3 rolls. DP.

Records of the Nevada Superintendency of Indian Affairs, 1869–1870.
M837. 1 roll. DP.

Records of the New Mexico Superintendency of Indian Affairs, 1849–1880.
T21. 30 rolls.8.

Records of the Northern Superintendency of Indian Affairs, 1851–1876.
M1166. 35 rolls. DP.

Records of the Oregon Superintendency of Indian Affairs, 1848–1873.
M2. 29 rolls. DP.

Records of the Southern Superintendency of Indian Affairs, 1832–1870.
M640. 22 rolls. DP.

Records of the Utah Superintendency of Indian Affairs, 1853–1870.
M834. 2 rolls. DP.

Records of the Washington Superintendency of Indian Affairs, 1853–1874.
M5. 26 rolls. DP.

Records of the Wisconsin Superintendency of Indian Affairs, 1836–1848, and the Green Bay Subagency, 1850.
M951. 4 rolls. DP.

Records of Boundary and Claims Commissions and Arbitrations. RG 76.

Records Relating to the First Northwest Boundary Survey Commission, 1853–1869.
T606. 4 rolls.

Records Relating to Claims Against Brazil Under the Convention of 1849.
T1187. 19 rolls.

Records of and Relating to the C.S.S. *Florida*, 1862–1864.
T716. 4 rolls.

Records of the Office of the Chief of Engineers. RG 77

Letters Sent by the Office of the Chief of Engineers Relating to Internal Improvements, 1824–1830.
M65.   3 rolls.   DP.

Letters Sent by the Topographical Bureau of the War Department and by Successor Divisions in the Office of the Chief of Engineers, 1829–1870.
M66.   37 rolls.   DP.

Buell Collection of Historical Documents Relating to the Corps of Engineers, 1801–1819.
M417.   3 rolls.   DP.

Registers of Letters Received by the Topographical Bureau of the War Department, 1824–1866.
M505.   4 rolls.   DP.

Letters Received by the Topographical Bureau of the War Department, 1824–1865.
M506.   86 rolls.   DP.

Harrison-Bundy Files Relating to the Development of the Atomic Bomb, 1942–1946.
M1108.   9 rolls.   DP.

Correspondence ("Top Secret") of the Manhattan Engineer District, 1942–1946.
M1109.   5 rolls.   DP.

Letters Sent by the Chief of Engineers, 1812–1869.
M1113.   8 rolls.

➤Name and Subject Index to Field Survey Records, 1793–1916.
M1702.   1 roll.

➤General Information Index to Names and Subjects ("The De Grange Index"), 1789–1889.
M1703.   7 rolls.

Records of the U.S. Naval Observatory. RG 78

Correspondence of the U.S. Naval Astronomical Expedition to the Southern Hemisphere, 1846–1861.
T54.   1 roll.

General Records of the Department of the Navy, 1798–1947. RG 80

Annual Reports of the Governors of Guam, 1901–1941.
M181.   3 rolls.   DP.

Annual Reports of Fleets and Task Forces of the U.S. Navy, 1920–1941.
M971.   15 rolls.   DP.

General and Special Indexes to the General Correspondence of the Office of the Secretary of the Navy, July 1897–Aug. 1926.
M1052.   119 rolls. DP.

Name and Subject Index to the General Correspondence of the Office of the Secretary of the Navy, 1930–1942.
M1067.   187 rolls. DP.

Indexes and Subject Cards to the "Secret and Confidential" Correspondence of the Office of the Secretary of the Navy, Mar. 1917–July 1919.
M1092.   11 rolls.   DP.

Secret and Confidential Correspondence of the Office of the Chief of Naval Operations and the Office of the Secretary of the Navy, 1919–1927.
M1140.   117 rolls. DP.

Indexes and Register to the Correspondence of the Office of the Chief of Naval Operations and the Office of the Secretary of the Navy, 1919–1927.
M1141.   9 rolls.   DP.

Proceedings of the General Board of the U.S. Navy, 1900–1950.
M1493.   28 rolls.   DP.

Records of the U.S. International Trade Commission. RG 81

U.S. Imports for Consumption, 1930–1938.
A1150.   41 rolls.

Records of the Federal Reserve System. RG 82

Minutes of the Federal Open Market Committee, 1936–1974, and of Its Executive Committee, 1936–1955.
M591.   43 rolls.   DP.

Records of the Foreign Service Posts of the Department of State. RG 84

Selected Records of U.S. Legations

Selected Records of the U.S. Legation in Chile, 1893–1905.
M20.   14 rolls.

Selected Records of the U.S. Legation in China, 1849–1931.
T898.   20 rolls.

Selected Records of the U.S. Legation in France, 1836–1842.
M14.   10 rolls.

Selected Records of the U.S. Legation in Japan, 1855–1912.
T400.   94 rolls.

Selected Records of the U.S. Legation in Paraguay, 1861–1907.
T693.   5 rolls.

Selected Records of the U.S. Legation in Peru, 1826–1912.
T724.   88 rolls.

Selected Records of U.S. Consular Posts

Selected Records of the U.S. Consulate in Bangkok, Siam, 1856–1912.
T403.   14 rolls.

Selected Records of the U.S. Consulate in Bombay, India, 1894–1912.
T307.   7 rolls.

Selected Records of the U.S. Consulate at Callao-Lima, Peru, 1825–1912.
T781.   73 rolls.

Selected Records of the U.S. Consulate in Kunming, China, 1922–1928.
T402.   19 rolls.

Selected Records of the U.S. Consulate in Madras, India, 1908–1912.
T308.   8 rolls.

Bound Volumes of the General Records of the U.S. Consulate at Yokohama, Japan, 1936–1939.
M1520.   22 rolls.   DP.

Records of the Immigration and Naturalization Service. RG 85

Passenger Lists, Crew Lists, and Indexes

See also: Records of the Bureau of Customs

Indexes to Passenger, Ship, and Crew Lists

Index to Passenger Lists of Vessels Arriving at Ports in Alabama, Florida, Georgia, and South Carolina, 1890–1924.
T517.   26 rolls.

Index (Soundex) to Passenger Lists of Vessels Arriving at Baltimore, Maryland, 1897–July 1952.
T520.   42 rolls.   16mm.

Book Indexes, Boston Passenger Lists, 1899–1940.
T790.   107 rolls.

Index to Passenger Lists of Vessels Arriving at Boston, Massachusetts, Jan. 1, 1902–June 30, 1906.
T521.   11 rolls.   16mm.

Index to Passenger Lists of Vessels Arriving at Boston, Massachusetts, July 1, 1906–Dec. 31, 1920.
T617.   11 rolls.   16mm.1.

Index to Passenger Lists of Vessels Arriving at Galveston, Texas, 1896–1906.
M1357.   3 rolls.   16mm.

Index to Passenger Lists of Vessels Arriving at Galveston, Texas, 1906–1951.
M1358.   7 rolls.   16mm.

Index to Passengers Arriving at Gulfport, Mississippi, Aug. 27, 1904–Aug. 28, 1954, and at Pascagoula, Mississippi, July 15, 1903–May 21, 1935.
T523.   1 roll.   16mm.

Index to Passengers Arriving at New Bedford, Massachusetts, July 1, 1902–Nov. 18, 1954.
T522.   2 rolls.   16mm.

Index to Passenger Lists of Vessels Arriving at New Orleans, Louisiana, 1900–1952.
T618.   22 rolls.   16mm.

Index to Passenger Lists of Vessels Arriving at New York, New York, June 16, 1897–June 30, 1902.
T519.   115 rolls.   16mm.

Book Indexes, New York Passenger Lists, 1906–1942.
T612.   807 rolls.

Index (Soundex) to Passenger Lists of Vessels Arriving at New York, New York, July 1, 1902–Dec. 31, 1943.
T621.   744 rolls.

Index (Soundex) to Passengers Arriving in New York, New York, 1944–1948.
M1417.   94 rolls.

Index (Soundex) Cards, Ship Arrivals at Philadelphia, Pennsylvania, Jan. 1, 1883–June 28, 1948.
T526.   60 rolls.   16mm.

Book Indexes, Philadelphia Passenger Lists, 1906–1926.
T791.   23 rolls.

Book Indexes, Portland, Maine, Passenger Lists, 1907–1930.
T793.   12 rolls.

Index to Passengers Arriving at Portland, Maine, Jan. 29, 1893–Nov. 22, 1954.
T524.   1 roll.   16mm.

Book Indexes, Providence Passenger Lists, 1911–1934.
T792.   15 rolls.

Index to Passengers Arriving at Providence, Rhode Island, June 18, 1911–Oct. 5, 1954.
T518.   2 rolls.2.

Soundex Index to Canadian Border Entries through the St. Albans, Vermont, District, 1895–1924.
M1461.   400 rolls.   16mm.

Soundex Index to Entries into the St. Albans, Vermont, District through Canadian Pacific and Atlantic Ports, 1924–1952.
M1463.   98 rolls.   16mm.

Indexes to Passenger Lists of Vessels Arriving at San Francisco, California, 1893–1934.
M1389.   28 rolls.   16mm.

Indexes to Vessels Arriving at San Francisco, 1882–1957.
M1437.   1 roll.

Passenger Lists

Passenger Lists of Vessels Arriving at Baltimore, Maryland, 1891–1909.
T844.   150 rolls.

Passenger Lists of Vessels Arriving at Boston, Massachusetts, 1891–1943.
T843.   454 rolls.

Card Manifests (Alphabetical) of Individuals Entering through the Port of Detroit, Michigan, 1906–54.
M1478.   117 rolls.

Passenger and Alien Crew Lists of Vessels Arriving at the Port of Detroit, Michigan, 1946–57.
M1479.   23 rolls.

Passenger Lists of Vessels Arriving at Galveston, Texas, 1896–1951.
M1359.   36 rolls.

Passenger Lists of Vessels Arriving at Key West, Florida, 1898–1945.
T940.   122 rolls.

Passenger Lists of Vessels Arriving at New Bedford, Massachusetts, 1902–1942.
T944.   8 rolls.

Passenger Lists of Vessels Arriving at New Orleans, Louisiana, 1903–1945.
T905.   189 rolls.

Passenger and Crew Lists of Vessels Arriving at New York, New York, 1897–1957.
T715.   8,892 rolls.

Passenger Lists of Vessels Arriving at Philadelphia, Pennsylvania, 1883–1945.
T840.   181 rolls.

Passenger Lists of Vessels Arriving at Portland, Maine, Nov. 29, 1893–Mar. 1943.
A1151.   35 rolls.2.

Customs Passenger Lists of Vessels Arriving at Port Townsend and Tacoma, Washington, 1894–1909.
M1484.   1 roll.   DP.

Passenger Lists of Vessels Arriving at Providence, Rhode Island, 1911–1943.
A1188.   49 rolls.

Manifests of Passengers Arriving in the St. Albans, Vermont, District through Canadian Pacific Ports, 1929–1949.
M1465.   25 rolls.

Lists of Chinese Passenger Arrivals at San Francisco, 1882–1914.
M1414.   32 rolls.

Passenger Lists of Vessels Arriving at San Francisco, 1893–1953.
M1410.   429 rolls.

Passenger Lists of Vessels Arriving at San Francisco from Honolulu, 1902–1907.
M1494.   1 roll.

Customs Passenger Lists of Vessels Arriving at San Francisco, 1903–1918.
M1412.   13 rolls.

Passenger Lists of Vessels Arriving at San Francisco from Insular Possessions, 1907–1911.
M1438.   2 rolls.

Passenger and Crew Lists of Vessels Arriving at San Francisco, 1954–1957.
M1411.   19 rolls.

Passenger Lists of Vessels Arriving at Savannah, Georgia, 1906–1945.
T943.   4 rolls.

Lists of Chinese Passengers Arriving at Seattle (Port Townsend), Washington, 1882–1916.
M1364.   10 rolls.

Passenger and Crew Lists of Vessels Arriving at Seattle, Washington, 1890–1957.
M1383.   357 rolls.

Passenger Lists of Vessels Arriving at Seattle from Insular Possessions, 1908–1917.
M1485.   1 roll.

Passenger Lists of Vessels Arriving at Seattle, Washington, 1949–1954.
M1398.   5 rolls.

Crew Lists

Crew Lists of Vessels Arriving at Boston, Massachusetts, 1917–1943.
T938.   269 rolls.

Crew Lists of Vessels Arriving at Gloucester, Massachusetts, 1918–1943.
T941.   13 rolls.

Crew Lists of Vessels Arriving at New Bedford, Massachusetts, 1917–1943.
T942.   2 rolls.

Crew Lists of Vessels Arriving at New Orleans, Louisiana, 1910–1945.
T939.   311 rolls.

Admitted Alien Crew Lists of Vessels Arriving at San Francisco, 1896–1921.
M1436.   8 rolls.

Crew Lists of Vessels Arriving at San Francisco, 1905–1954.
M1416.   174 rolls.

Crew Lists of Vessels Arriving at Seattle, Washington, 1903–1917.
M1399.   15 rolls.
See also Passenger Lists.

Other Records

Subject Index to Correspondence and Case Files of the Immigration and Naturalization Service, 1903–1952.
T458.   31 rolls.

➤Index to New England Naturalization Records, 1791–1906.
M1299.   117 rolls.

Case Files of Chinese Immigrants, 1895–1920, From District No. 4 (Philadelphia) of the Immigration and Naturalization Service.
M1144.   51 rolls.   DP.

Records of the Special Boards of Inquiry, District No. 4 (Philadelphia), Immigration and Naturalization Service, 1893–1909.
M1500.   18 rolls.   DP.

Minutes of the Boards of Special Inquiry at the San Francisco Immigration Office, 1899–1909.
M1387.   2 rolls.

Registers of Chinese Laborers Returning to the U.S. through the Port of San Francisco, 1882–1888.
M1413.   12 rolls.

Lists of U.S. Citizens Arriving at San Francisco, 1930–1949.
M1439.   50 rolls.

Lists of Chinese Applying for Admission to the United States Through the Port of San Francisco, 1903–1947.
M1476.   27 rolls.

➤Soundex Index to Naturalization Petitions for the United States District and Circuit Courts, Northern District of Illinois, and Immigration and Naturalization Service District 9, 1840–1950.
M1285.   179 rolls.   DP.

Certificates of Head Tax Paid by Aliens Arriving at Seattle from Foreign Contiguous Territory, 1917–1924.
M1365.   10 rolls.

Alphabetical Index to Canadian Border Entries through Small Ports in Vermont, 1895–1924.
M1462.   6 rolls.

Manifest of Passengers Arriving in the St. Albans, Vermont, District through Canadian Pacific and Atlantic Ports, 1895–1954.
M1464.   639 rolls.

➤Immigration and Naturalization Service Case Files of Chinese Immigrants, Portland, Oregon, 1890–1914.
M1638.   15 rolls.

Records of the U.S. Secret Service. RG 87

Register of Monthly Reports by U.S. Secret Service Agents, Dec. 1864–Feb. 1871.
T917.   7 rolls.

Daily Reports of U.S. Secret Service Agents, 1875–1936.
T915.   836 rolls.

Records of the Public Health Service, 1912–1968. RG 90

Letters Received by the National Board of Health, 1879–1884, and Related Register, 1879–1882.
M753.   59 rolls.   DP.

Records of the Office of the Quartermaster General. RG 92

Letters Sent by the Office of the Quartermaster General, Main Series, 1818–1870.
M745.   61 rolls.   DP.

Register of Confederate Soldiers, Sailors, and Citizens who Died in Federal Prisons and Military Hospitals in the North, 1861–1865.
M918.   1 roll.   DP.

➤Selected Records of the National Military Cemetery at Fayetteville, Arkansas, 1867–1914.
M1780.   1 roll.

War Department Collection of Revolutionary War Records. RG 93

Indexes to Compiled Service Records

General Index to Compiled Military Service Records of Revolutionary War Soldiers.
M860.   58 rolls. DP.   16mm.

Index to Compiled Service Records of American Naval Personnel who Served During the Revolutionary War.
M879.   1 roll.   DP.

Index to Compiled Service Records of Revolutionary War Soldiers who Served With the American Army in Connecticut Military Organizations.
M920.   25 rolls. DP.

Index to Compiled Service Records of Revolutionary War Soldiers who Served With the American Army in Georgia Military Organizations.
M1051. 1 roll.   DP.

Index to Compiled Service Records of Volunteer Soldiers who Served During the Revolutionary War in Organizations From the State of North Carolina.
M257.   2 rolls.   DP.   16mm.

Compiled Service Records

Compiled Service Records of American Naval Personnel and Members of the Departments of the Quartermaster General and the Commissary General of Military Stores who Served During the Revolutionary War.
M880.   4 rolls.   DP.

Compiled Service Records of Soldiers who Served in the American Army During the Revolutionary War.
M881.   1,096 rolls.   DP.

Other Records

Revolutionary War Rolls, 1775–1783.
M246.   138 rolls. DP.

Special Index to Numbered Records in the War Department Collection of Revolutionary War Records, 1775–1783.
M847.   39 rolls. DP.

Numbered Record Books Concerning Military Operations and Service, Pay and Settlement of Accounts, and Supplies in the War Department Collection of Revolutionary War Records.
M853.   41 rolls. DP.

Miscellaneous Numbered Records (The Manuscript File) in the War Department Collection of Revolutionary War Records, 1775–1790's.
M859.   125 rolls. DP.

Personnel Returns of the 6th Massachusetts Battalion, 1779–1780, and Returns and Accounts of Military Stores for the 8th and 9th Massachusetts Regiments, 1779–1782.
M913.   1 roll.   DP.

Orders, Returns, Morning Reports, and Accounts of British Troops, 1776–1781.
M922.   1 roll.   DP.

Letters, Returns, Accounts, and Estimates of the Quartermaster General's Department, 1776–1783, in the War Department Collection of Revolutionary War Records.
M926.   1 roll.   DP.

General Orders Kept by Gen. William Heath, May 23, 1777–Oct. 20, 1778.
T42.   1 roll.

Records of the Adjutant General's Office, 1780's–1917. RG 94

Correspondence

Index to General Correspondence of the Office of the Adjutant General, 1890–1917.
M698.   1,269 rolls.   DP.

Indexes to Letters Received by the Office of the Adjutant General (Main Series), 1846, 1861–1889.
M725.   9 rolls.   DP.

Registers of Letters Received, Office of the Adjutant General, 1812–1889.
M711.   85 rolls. DP.

Letters Received by the Office of the Adjutant General, 1805–1821.
M566.   144 rolls. DP.

Letters Received by the Office of the Adjutant General (Main Series), 1822–1860.
M567.   636 rolls. DP.

Letters Received by the Office of the Adjutant General (Main Series), 1861–1870.
M619.   828 rolls. DP.

Letters Received by the Office of the Adjutant General (Main Series), 1871–1880.
M666   593 rolls. DP.

Letters Received by the Office of the Adjutant General (Main Series), 1881–1889.
M689.   740 rolls. DP.

Letters Sent by the Office of the Adjutant General (Main Series), 1800–1890.
M565.   63 rolls.   DP.

Indexes to Compiled Service Records

1784–Mexican War

Index to Compiled Service Records of Volunteer Soldiers who Served From 1784–1811.
M694.   9 rolls.   DP.   16mm.

Index to Compiled Service Records of Volunteer Soldiers who Served During the War of 1812.
M602.   234 rolls. DP.   16mm.

Index to Compiled Service Records of Volunteer Soldiers who Served During the War of 1812 in Organizations From the State of Louisiana.
M229.   3 rolls.   DP.   16mm.

Index to Compiled Service Records of Volunteer Soldiers who Served During the War of 1812 in Organizations From the State of North Carolina.
M250.   5 rolls.   DP.   16mm.

Index to Compiled Service Records of Volunteer Soldiers who Served During the War of 1812 in Organizations From the State of South Carolina.
M652.   7 rolls.   DP.   16mm.

Index to Compiled Service Records of Volunteer Soldiers who Served During Indian Wars and Disturbances, 1815–1858.
M629.   42 rolls.   DP.   16mm.

Index to Compiled Service Records of Volunteer Soldiers who Served During the Cherokee Removal in Organizations From the State of Alabama.
M243.   1 roll.   DP.   16mm.

Index to Compiled Service Records of Volunteer Soldiers who Served During the Cherokee Disturbances and Removal in Organizations From the State of Georgia.
M907.   1 roll.   DP.   16mm.

Index to Compiled Service Records of Volunteer Soldiers who Served During the Cherokee Disturbances and Removal in Organizations From the State of North Carolina.
M256.   1 roll.   DP.   16mm.

Index to Compiled Service Records of Volunteer Soldiers who Served During the Cherokee Disturbances and Removal in Organizations From the State of Tennessee and the Field and Staff of the Army of the Cherokee Nation.
M908.   2 rolls.   DP.   16mm.

Index to Compiled Service Records of Volunteer Soldiers who Served During the Creek War in Organizations From the State of Alabama.
M244.   2 rolls.   DP.   16mm.

Index to Compiled Service Records of Volunteer Soldiers who Served During the Florida War in Organizations From the State of Alabama.
M245.   1 roll.   DP.   16mm.

Index to Compiled Service Records of Volunteer Soldiers who Served During the Florida War in Organizations From the State of Louisiana.
M239.   1 roll.   DP.   16mm.

Index to Compiled Service Records of Volunteer Soldiers who Served During the War of 1837–1838 in Organizations From the State of Louisiana.
M241.   1 roll.   DP.   16mm.

Index to Compiled Service Records of Volunteer Soldiers who Served From the State of Michigan During the Patriot War, 1838–1839.
M630.   1 roll.   DP.   16mm.

Index to Compiled Service Records of Volunteer Soldiers who Served From the State of New York During the Patriot War, 1838.
M631.   1 roll.   DP.   16mm.

Index to Compiled Service Records of Volunteer Soldiers who Served During the Mexican War.
M616.   41 rolls.   DP.   16mm.

Civil War

Alphabetical Card Name Indexes to the Compiled Service Records of Volunteer Soldiers who Served in Union Organizations not Raised by States or Territories, Excepting the Veterans Reserve Corps and the U.S. Colored Troops.
M1290.   36 rolls.   DP.

Index to Compiled Service Records of Volunteer Union Soldiers who Served in Organizations From the State of Alabama.
M263.   1 roll.   DP.   16mm.

Index to Compiled Service Records of Volunteer Union Soldiers who Served in Organizations From the Territory of Arizona.
M532.   1 roll.   DP.   16mm.

Index to Compiled Service Records of Volunteer Union Soldiers who Served in Organizations From the State of Arkansas.
M383.   4 rolls.   DP.   16mm.

Index to Compiled Service Records of Volunteer Union Soldiers who Served in Organizations From the State of California.
M533.   7 rolls.   DP.   16mm.

Index to Compiled Service Records of Volunteer Union Soldiers who Served in Organizations From the Territory of Colorado.
M534.   3 rolls.   DP.   16mm.

Index to Compiled Service Records of Volunteer Union Soldiers who Served in Organizations From the State of Connecticut.
M535.   17 rolls.   DP.   16mm.

Index to Compiled Service Records of Volunteer Union Soldiers who Served in Organizations From the Territory of Dakota.
M536.   1 roll.   DP.   16mm.

Index to Compiled Service Records of Volunteer Union Soldiers who Served in Organizations From the State of Delaware.
M537.   4 rolls.   DP.   16mm.

Index to Compiled Service Records of Volunteer Union Soldiers who Served in Organizations From the District of Columbia.
M538.   3 rolls.   DP.   16mm.

Index to Compiled Service Records of Volunteer Union Soldiers who Served in Organizations From the State of Florida.
M264.   1 roll.   DP.   16mm.

Index to Compiled Service Records of Volunteer Union Soldiers who Served in Organizations From the State of Georgia.
M385.   1 roll.   DP.   16mm.

Index to Compiled Service Records of Volunteer Union Soldiers who Served in Organizations From the State of Illinois.
M539.   101 rolls. DP.   16mm.

Index to Compiled Service Records of Volunteer Union Soldiers who Served in Organizations From the State of Indiana.
M540.   86 rolls.   DP.   16mm.

Index to Compiled Service Records of Volunteer Union Soldiers who Served in Organizations From the State of Iowa.
M541.   29 rolls.   DP.   16mm.

Index to Compiled Service Records of Volunteer Union Soldiers who Served in Organizations From the State of Kansas.
M542.   10 rolls.   DP.   16mm.

Index to Compiled Service Records of Volunteer Union Soldiers who Served in Organizations From the State of Kentucky.
M386.   30 rolls.   DP.   16mm.

Index to Compiled Service Records of Volunteer Union Soldiers who Served in Organizations From the State of Louisiana.
M387.   4 rolls.   DP.   16mm.

Index to Compiled Service Records of Volunteer Union Soldiers who Served in Organizations From the State of Maine.
M543.   23 rolls.   DP.   16mm.

Index to Compiled Service Records of Volunteer Union Soldiers who Served in Organizations From the State of Maryland.
M388. 13 rolls. DP. 16mm.

Index to Compiled Service Records of Volunteer Union Soldiers who Served in Organizations From the State of Massachusetts.
M544. 44 rolls. DP. 16mm.

Index to Compiled Service Records of Volunteer Union Soldiers who Served in Organizations From the State of Michigan.
M545. 48 rolls. DP. 16mm.

Index to Compiled Service Records of Volunteer Union Soldiers who Served in Organizations From the State of Minnesota.
M546. 10 rolls. DP. 16mm.

Index to Compiled Service Records of Volunteer Union Soldiers who Served in Organizations From the State of Mississippi.
M389. 1 roll. DP. 16mm.

Index to Compiled Service Records of Volunteer Union Soldiers who Served in Organizations From the State of Missouri.
M390. 54 rolls. DP. 16mm.

Index to Compiled Service Records of Volunteer Union Soldiers who Served in Organizations From the Territory of Nebraska.
M547. 2 rolls. DP. 16mm.

Index to Compiled Service Records of Volunteer Union Soldiers who Served in Organizations From the State of Nevada.
M548. 1 roll. DP. 16mm.

Index to Compiled Service Records of Volunteer Union Soldiers who Served in Organizations From the State of New Hampshire.
M549. 13 rolls. DP. 16mm.

Index to Compiled Service Records of Volunteer Union Soldiers who Served in Organizations From the State of New Jersey.
M550. 26 rolls. DP. 16mm.

Index to Compiled Service Records of Volunteer Union Soldiers who Served in Organizations From the Territory of New Mexico.
M242. 4 rolls. DP. 16mm.

Index to Compiled Service Records of Volunteer Union Soldiers who Served in Organizations From the State of New York.
M551. 157 rolls. DP. 16mm.

Index to Compiled Service Records of Volunteer Union Soldiers who Served in Organizations From the State of North Carolina.
M391. 2 rolls. DP. 16mm.

Index to Compiled Service Records of Volunteer Union Soldiers who Served in Organizations From the State of Ohio.
M552. 122 rolls. DP. 16mm.

Index to Compiled Service Records of Volunteer Union Soldiers who Served in Organizations From the State of Oregon.
M553. 1 roll. DP. 16mm.

Index to Compiled Service Records of Volunteer Union Soldiers who Served in Organizations From the State of Pennsylvania.
M554. 136 rolls. DP. 16mm.

Index to Compiled Service Records of Volunteer Union Soldiers who Served in Organizations From the State of Rhode Island.
M555. 7 rolls. DP. 16mm.

Index to Compiled Service Records of Volunteer Union Soldiers who Served in Organizations From the State of Tennessee.
M392. 16 rolls. DP. 16mm.

Index to Compiled Service Records of Volunteer Union Soldiers who Served in Organizations From the State of Texas.
M393. 2 rolls. DP. 16mm.

Index to Compiled Service Records of Volunteer Union Soldiers who Served in Organizations From the Territory of Utah.
M556. 1 roll. DP. 16mm.

Index to Compiled Service Records of Volunteer Union Soldiers who Served in Organizations From the State of Vermont.
M557. 14 rolls. DP. 16mm.

Index to Compiled Service Records of Volunteer Union Soldiers who Served in Organizations From the State of Virginia.
M394. 1 roll. DP. 16mm.

Index to Compiled Service Records of Volunteer Union Soldiers who Served in Organizations From the Territory of Washington.
M558. 1 roll. DP. 16mm.

Index to Compiled Service Records of Volunteer Union Soldiers who Served in Organizations From the State of West Virginia.
M507. 13 rolls. DP. 16mm.

Index to Compiled Service Records of Volunteer Union Soldiers who Served in Organizations From the State of Wisconsin.
M559. 33 rolls. DP. 16mm.

Index to Compiled Service Records of Volunteer Union Soldiers who Served in the Veteran Reserve Corps.
M636. 44 rolls. DP. 16mm.

Index to Compiled Service Records of Volunteer Union Soldiers who Served With U.S. Colored Troops.
M589. 98 rolls. DP. 16mm.

War With Spain and Philippine Insurrection

General Index to Compiled Service Records of Volunteer Soldiers who Served During the War With Spain.
M871. 126 rolls. DP. 16mm.

Index to Compiled Service Records of Volunteer Soldiers who Served During the War With Spain in Organizations From the State of Louisiana.
M240. 1 roll. DP. 16mm.

Index to Compiled Service Records of Volunteer Soldiers who Served During the War With Spain in Organizations From the State of North Carolina.
M413. 2 rolls. DP. 16mm.

Index to Compiled Service Records of Volunteer Soldiers who Served During the Philippine Insurrection.
M872. 24 rolls. DP. 16mm.

Compiled Service Records of Volunteer Soldiers

1784–Mexican War

Compiled Service Records of Volunteer Soldiers who Served From 1784 to 1811.
M905. 32 rolls. DP. 16mm.

Compiled Service Records of Volunteer Soldiers who Served During the War of 1812 in Organizations From the Territory of Mississippi.
M678.   22 rolls. DP.   16mm.

Compiled Military Service Records of Michigan and Illinois Volunteers who Served During the Winnebago Indian Disturbances of 1827.
M1505.   3 rolls. DP.

Compiled Service Records of Volunteer Soldiers who Served in Organizations From the State of Florida During the Florida Indian Wars, 1835–1858.
M1086.   63 rolls. DP.

Compiled Service Records of Volunteer Soldiers who Served During the Mexican War in Mormon Organizations.
M351.   3 rolls. DP.   16mm.

Compiled Service Records of Volunteer Soldiers who Served During the Mexican War in Organizations From the State of Mississippi.
M863.   9 rolls. DP.   16mm.

Compiled Service Records of Volunteer Soldiers who Served During the Mexican War in Organizations From the State of Pennsylvania.
M1028.   13 rolls. DP.

Compiled Service Records of Volunteer Soldiers who Served During the Mexican War in Organizations From the State of Tennessee.
M638.   15 rolls. DP.   16mm.

Compiled Service Records of Volunteer Soldiers who Served During the Mexican War in Organizations From the State of Texas.
M278.   19 rolls. DP.   16mm.

Civil War

Compiled Service Records of Volunteer Union Soldiers who Served in Organizations From the State of Alabama.
M276.   10 rolls. DP.   16mm.

Compiled Service Records of Volunteer Union Soldiers who Served in Organizations From the State of Arkansas.
M399.   60 rolls. DP.   16mm.

Compiled Service Records of Volunteer Union Soldiers who Served in Organizations From the State of Florida.
M400.   11 rolls. DP.   16mm.

Compiled Service Records of Volunteer Union Soldiers who Served in Organizations From the State of Georgia.
M403.   1 roll. DP.   16mm.

Compiled Service Records of Volunteeer Union Soldiers who Served in Organizations From the State of Kentucky.
M397.   515 rolls. DP.   16mm.

Compiled Service Records of Volunteer Union Soldiers who Served in Organizations From the State of Louisiana.
M396.   50 rolls. DP.   16mm.

Compiled Service Records of Volunteer Union Soldiers who Served in Organizations From the State of Maryland.
M384.   238 rolls. DP.   16mm.

Compiled Service Records of Volunteer Union Soldiers who Served in Organizations From the State of Mississippi.
M404.   4 rolls. DP.   16mm.

Compiled Service Records of Volunteer Union Soldiers who Served in Organizations From the State of Missouri.
M405.   854 rolls. DP.   16mm.

►Compiled Service Records of Volunteer Union Soldiers Who Served in Organizations from the Territory of Nebraska.
M1787.   43 rolls. DP.

Compiled Service Records of Volunteer Union Soldiers who Served in Organizations From the Territory of New Mexico.
M427.   46 rolls. DP.   16mm.

Compiled Service Records of Volunteer Union Soldiers who Served in Organizations From the State of North Carolina.
M401.   25 rolls. DP.   16mm.

Compiled Service Records of Volunteer Union Soldiers who Served in Organizations From the State of Tennessee.
M395.   220 rolls. DP.   16mm.

Compiled Service Records of Volunteer Union Soldiers who Served in Organizations From the State of Texas.
M402.   13 rolls. DP.   16mm.

Compiled Service Records of Volunteer Union Soldiers who Served in Organizations From the Territory of Utah.
M692.   1 roll. DP.   16mm.

Compiled Service Records of Volunteer Union Soldiers who Served in Organizations From the State of Virginia.
M398.   7 rolls. DP.   16mm.

Compiled Service Records of Volunteer Union Soldiers who Served in Organizations From the State of West Virgina.
M508.   261 rolls. DP.   16mm.

Compiled Service Records of Former Confederate Soldiers who Served in the 1st Through 6th U.S. Volunteer Infantry Regiments, 1864–1866.
M1017.   65 rolls. DP.

War With Spain

Compiled Service Records of Volunteer Soldiers who Served in the Florida Infantry During the War With Spain.
M1087.   13 rolls. DP.

Other Records

Orders of Gen. Zachary Taylor to the Army of Occupation in the Mexican War, 1845–1847.
M29.   3 rolls.

Records Relating to the U.S. Military Academy, 1812–1867.
M91.   29 rolls. DP.

Letters Sent by the Governors and the Secretary of State of California, 1847–1848.
M182.   1 roll. DP.

Register of Enlistments in the U.S. Army, 1798–1914.
M233.   81 rolls.

Compiled Records Showing Service of Military Units in Volunteer Union Organizations.
M594.   225 rolls. DP.   16mm.

Gen. James Wilkinson's Order Book, Dec. 31, 1796–Mar. 8, 1808.
M654.   3 rolls. DP.   16mm.

Returns From U.S. Military Posts, 1800–1916.
M617.   1,550 rolls.   DP.

Historical Information Relating to
Military Posts and Other Installations,
ca. 1700–1900.
M661.   8 rolls.   DP.

Returns From Regular Army Infantry
Regiments, June 1821–Dec. 1916.
M665.   300 rolls. DP.

Index to General Correspondence of the
Record and Pension Office, 1889–1920.
M686.   385 rolls. DP.   16mm.

U.S. Military Academy Cadet
Application Papers, 1805–1866.
M688.   242 rolls. DP.

Returns From Regular Army Engineer
Battalions, Sept. 1846–June 1916.
M690.   10 rolls.   DP.

Returns From Regular Army Coast
Artillery Corps Companies, Feb.
1901–June 1916.
M691.   81 rolls.   DP.

*History of the Philippine Insurrection
Against the United States, 1899–1903*,
and Documents Relating to the War
Department Project for Publishing the
History.
M719.   9 rolls.   DP.

Returns From Regular Army Artillery
Regiments, June 1821–Jan. 1901.
M727.   38 rolls.   DP.

Returns From Regular Army Field
Artillery Batteries and Regiments,
Feb. 1901–Dec. 1916.
M728.   14 rolls.   DP.

Case Files of Investigations by
Levi C. Turner and Lafayette C. Baker,
1861–1866.
M797.   137 rolls.   DP.

Official Battle Lists of the Civil War,
1861–1865.
M823.   2 rolls.   DP.

Returns of the Corps of Engineers,
Apr. 1832–Dec. 1916.
M851.   22 rolls.   DP.

Returns of the Corps of Topographical
Engineers, Nov. 1831–Feb. 1863.
M852.   2 rolls.   DP.

The Negro in the Military Service of the
United States, 1639–1886.
M858.   5 rolls.   DP.

War Department Collection of Post-
Revolutionary War Manuscripts.
M904.   4 rolls.   DP.

Reports and Correspondence
Relating to the Army Investigations
of the Battle of Wounded Knee and
to the Sioux Campaign of
1890–1891.
M983.   2 rolls.   DP.

Pardon Petitions and Related Papers
Submitted in Response to President
Andrew Johnson's Amnesty
Proclamation of May 29, 1865
("Amnesty Papers").
M1003.   73 rolls.   DP.

Letters Received by the Commission
Branch of the Adjutant General's
Office, 1863–1870.
M1064.   527 rolls. DP.

General Orders and Circulars of the
War Department and Headquarters of
the Army, 1809–1860.
M1094.   8 rolls.   DP.

U.S. Army Generals' Reports of Civil
War Service, 1864–1887.
M1098.   8 rolls.   DP.

Name and Subject Index to the Letters
Received by the Appointment,
Commission, and Personal Branch
of the Adjutant General's Office,
1871–1894.
M1125.   4 rolls.   DP.

Records Relating to the 1811 and
1815 Courts-Martial of Maj. Gen.
James Wilkinson.
M1136.   2 rolls.   DP.7.

Proceedings of U.S. Army Courts-
martial and Military Commissions of
Union Soldiers Executed by U.S.
Military Authorities, 1861–1866.
M1523.   8 rolls.   DP.

➤Index to Records Relating to War of
1812 Prisoners of War.
M1747.   3 rolls.

➤Records of the Fifty-fourth
Massachusetts Infantry Regiment
(Colored), 1863–1865.
M1659.   7 rolls.   DP.

Lt. Zebulon Pike's Notebook of Maps,
Traverse Tables, and Meteorological
Observations, 1805–1807.
T36.   1 roll.

Lists of the Adjutant General's Office
for Carded Records of Military
Organizations: Revolutionary War
through Philippine Insurrection
("The Ainsworth List").
T817.   112 rolls.

Muster Rolls and Payrolls of Militia and
Regular Army Organizations in the
Battle of Tippecanoe, Nov. 1811.
T1085.   1 roll.

*Artillery for the U.S. Land Service With
Plates*, by Bvt. Maj. Alfred Mordecai
(Washington, 1848–1849).
T1104.   1 roll.

Publications of the Office of Military
History, U.S. Army, American Forces in
Action.
T1107.   3 rolls.

Publications of the Office of Military
History, U.S. Army, Department of the
Army Pamphlets.
T1108.   7 rolls.

*Cavalry Tactics, U.S. Army,
Assimilated to the Tactics of Infantry
and Artillery* (New York, 1874).
T1109   1 roll.

Orders and Special Orders by Maj.
Gen. William O. Butler and Maj. Gen.
W. J. Worth to the Army in Mexico,
1848.
T1114   1 roll.

Orders Issued by Brig. Gen. Stephen
W. Kearney and Brig. Gen. Sterling
Price to the Army of the West, 1846–
1848.
T1115.   1 roll.

*The Ordnance Manual for the Officers
of the U.S. Army* (3rd ed.,
Philadelphia, 1862).
T1117.   1 roll.

Records of the Forest Service. RG 95

Minutes of the Service Committee of
the Forest Service, Mar. 14, 1903–Oct.
16, 1935.
M1025.   8 rolls.   DP.

Shelf List of Captions for the General
Photograph File, U.S. Forest Service.
M1128.   27 rolls.   16mm.

General Photographic File of the U.S.
Forest Service, 1886–.
M1127.   121 rolls.

Records of the Office of the Comptroller of the Currency. RG 101

Registers of Signatures of Depositors in Branches of the Freedman's Savings and Trust Company, 1865–1874.
M816.   27 rolls.   DP.

Indexes to Deposit Ledgers in Branches of the Freedman's Savings and Trust Company, 1865–1874.
M817.   5 rolls.   DP.

Journal of the Board of Trustees and Minutes of Committees and Inspectors of the Freedman's Savings and Trust Company, 1865–1874.
M874.   2 rolls.   DP.

Records of the Farm Credit Administration. RG 103

Records of Farmers' Marketing and Purchasing Cooperatives.
T947.   38 rolls.

Records of the U.S. Mint. RG 104

Letters Sent by the Director of the U.S. Mint at Philadelphia, 1795–1817.
M64.   1 roll.   DP.

Bullion Ledgers of the U.S. Mint at Philadelphia, 1794–1802.
T587.   1 roll.

Correspondence of the U.S. Mint at Philadelphia With the Branch Mint at Dahlonega, Georgia, 1835–1861.
T646.   3 rolls.

Records of the Bureau of Refugees, Freedmen, and Abandoned Lands. RG 105

Selected Series of Records Issued by the Commissioner of the Bureau of Refugees, Freedmen, and Abandoned Lands, 1865–1872.
M742.   7 rolls.   DP.

Registers and Letters Received by the Commissioner of the Bureau of Refugees, Freedmen, and Abandoned Lands, 1865–1872.
M752.   74 rolls.   DP.

Records of the Education Division of the Bureau of Refugees, Freedmen, and Abandoned Lands, 1865–1871.
M803.   35 rolls.   DP.

Records of the Assistant Commissioner for the State of Alabama, Bureau of Refugees, Freedmen, and Abandoned Lands, 1865–1870.
M809.   23 rolls.   DP.

Records of the Superintendent of Education for the State of Alabama, Bureau of Refugees, Freedmen, and Abandoned Lands, 1865–1870.
M810.   8 rolls.   DP.

Records of the Assistant Commissioner for the State of Arkansas, Bureau of Refugees, Freedmen, and Abandoned Lands, 1865–1869.
M979.   52 rolls.   DP.

Records of the Superintendent of Education for the State of Arkansas, Bureau of Refugees, Freedmen, and Abandoned Lands, 1865–1871.
M980.   5 rolls.   DP.

Records of the Assistant Commissioner for the District of Columbia, Bureau of Refugees, Freedmen, and Abandoned Lands, 1865–1872.
M1055.   21 rolls.   DP.

Records of the Superintendent of Education for the District of Columbia, Bureau of Refugees, Freedmen, and Abandoned Lands, 1865–1872.
M1056.   24 rolls.   DP.

Records of the Assistant Commissioner for the State of Georgia, Bureau of Refugees, Freedmen, and Abandoned Lands.
M798.   36 rolls.   DP.

Records of the Superintendent of Education for the State of Georgia, Bureau of Refugees, Freedmen, and Abandoned Lands, 1865–1870.
M799.   28 rolls.   DP.

Records of the Assistant Commissioner for the State of Louisiana, Bureau of Refugees, Freedmen, and Abandoned Lands, 1865–1869.
M1027.   37 rolls.   DP.

Records of the Superintendent of Education for the State of Louisiana, Bureau of Refugees, Freedmen, and Abandoned Lands, 1864–1869.
M1026.   12 rolls.   DP.

Records of the New Orleans Field Offices, Bureau of Refugees, Freedmen, and Abandoned Lands, 1865–69.
M1483.   10 rolls.   DP.

Records of the Assistant Commissioner for the State of Mississippi, Bureau of Refugees, Freedmen, and Abandoned Lands, 1865–1869.
M826.   50 rolls.   DP.

Records of the Assistant Commissioner for the State of North Carolina, Bureau of Refugees, Freedmen, and Abandoned Lands, 1865–1870.
M843.   38 rolls.   DP.

Records of the Superintendent of Education for the State of North Carolina, Bureau of Refugees, Freedmen, and Abandoned Lands, 1865–1870.
M844.   16 rolls.   DP.

Records of the Assistant Commissioner for the State of South Carolina, Bureau of Refugees, Freedmen, and Abandoned Lands, 1865–1870.
M869.   44 rolls.   DP.

Records of the Assistant Commissioner for the State of Tennessee, Bureau of Refugees, Freedmen, and Abandoned Lands, 1865–1869.
M999.   34 rolls.   DP.

Records of the Superintendent of Education for the State of Tennessee, Bureau of Refugees, Freedmen, and Abandoned Lands, 1865–1870.
M1000.   9 rolls.   DP.

Selected Records of the Tennessee Field Office of the Bureau of Refugees, Freedmen, and Abandoned Lands, 1865–1872.
T142.   73 rolls.

Records of the Assistant Commissioner for the State of Texas, Bureau of Refugees, Freedmen, and Abandoned Lands, 1865–1869.
M821.   32 rolls.   DP.

Records of the Superintendent of Education for the State of Texas, Bureau of Refugees, Freedmen, and Abandoned Lands, 1865–1870.
M822.   18 rolls.   DP.

Records of the Assistant Commissioner for the State of Virginia, Bureau of Refugees, Freedmen, and Abandoned Lands, 1865–1869.
M1048.   67 rolls.   DP.

Records of the Superintendent of Education for the State of Virginia, Bureau of Refugees, Freedmen, and Abandoned Lands, 1865–1870.
M1053.   20 rolls.   DP.

Records of the Office of the Secretary of War. RG 107

Registers of Letters Received by the Office of the Secretary of War, Main Series, 1800–1870.
M22.   134 rolls.   DP.

Registers of Letters Received by the Secretary of War, Irregular Series, 1861–1866.
M491.   4 rolls.   DP.

Registers of Letters Received by the Secretary of War From the President, Executive Departments, and War Department Bureaus, 1862–1870.
M493.   12 rolls.   DP.

Indexes to Letters Received by the Secretary of War, 1861–1870.
M495.   14 rolls.   DP.

Indexes to Letters Sent by the Secretary of War Relating to Military Affairs, 1871–1889.
M420.   12 rolls.   DP.

Index to Telegrams Collected by the Office of the Secretary of War (Unbound), 1860–1870.
M564.   20 rolls.   DP.   16mm.

Letters Received by the Secretary of War, Registered Series, 1801–1870.
M221.   317 rolls. DP.

Letters Received by the Secretary of War, Unregistered Series, 1789–1861.
M222.   34 rolls.   DP.

Letters Received by the Secretary of War, Irregular Series, 1861–1866.
M492.   36 rolls.   DP.

Letters Received by the Secretary of War From the President, Executive Departments, and War Department Bureaus, 1862–1870.
M494.   117 rolls. DP.

Letters Sent by the Secretary of War Relating to Military Affairs 1800–1889.
M6.   110 rolls. DP.

Miscellaneous Letters Sent by the Secretary of War, 1800–1809.
M370.   3 rolls.   DP.

Letters Sent to the President by the Secretary of War, 1800–1863.
M127.   6 rolls.   DP.

Letters Sent by the Secretary of War to the President and Executive Departments, 1863–1870.
M421.   5 rolls.   DP.

Confidential and Unofficial Letters Sent by the Secretary of War, 1814–1847.
M7.   2 rolls.   DP.

Telegrams Collected by the Office of the Secretary of War (Unbound), 1860–1870.
M504.   454 rolls. DP.

Telegrams Collected by the Office of the Secretary of War (Bound), 1861–1882.
M473.   282 rolls. DP.

Reports to Congress From the Secretary of War, 1803–1870.
M220.   5 rolls.   DP.

Orders and Endorsements Sent by the Secretary of War, 1846–1870.
M444.   13 rolls. DP.

Correspondence of the War Department Relating to Indian Affairs, Military Pensions, and Fortifications, 1791–1797.
M1062.   1 roll.   DP.

Records of the Headquarters of the Army. RG 108

Letters Sent by the Headquarters of the Army (Main Series), 1828–1903.
M857.   15 rolls.   DP.

➤Letters Received by the Headquarters of the Army, 1827–1903.
M1635.   139 rolls. DP.

War Department Collection of Confederate Records. RG 109

Indexes to Compiled Service Records

Consolidated Index to Compiled Service Records of Confederate Soldiers.
M253.   535 rolls. DP.   16mm.

Index to Compiled Service Records of Confederate Soldiers who Served in Organizations Raised Directly by the Confederate Government and of Confederate General and Staff Officers and Nonregimental Enlisted Men.
M818.   26 rolls.   DP.   16mm.

Index to Compiled Service Records of Confederate Soldiers who Served in Organizations From the State of Alabama.
M374.   49 rolls.   DP.   16mm.

Index to Compiled Service Records of Confederate Soldiers who Served in Organizations From the Territory of Arizona.
M375.   1 roll.   DP.   16mm.

Index to Compiled Service Records of Confederate Soldiers who Served in Organizations From the State of Arkansas.
M376.   26 rolls.   DP.   16mm.

Index to Compiled Service Records of Confederate Soldiers who Served in Organizations From the State of Florida.
M225.   9 rolls.   DP.   16mm.

Index to Compiled Service Records of Confederate Soldiers who Served in Organizations From the State of Georgia.
M226.   67 rolls.   DP.   16mm.

Index to Compiled Service Records of Confederate Soldiers who Served in Organizations From the State of Kentucky.
M377.   14 rolls.   DP.   16mm.

Index to Compiled Service Records of Confederate Soldiers who Served in Organizations From the State of Louisiana.
M378.   31 rolls.   DP.   16mm.

Index to Compiled Service Records of Confederate Soldiers who Served in Organizations From the State of Maryland.
M379.   2 rolls.   DP.   16mm.

Index to Compiled Service Records of Confederate Soldiers who Served in Organizations From the State of Mississippi.
M232.   45 rolls. DP.   16mm.

Index to Compiled Service Records of Confederate Soldiers who Served in Organizations From the State of Missouri.
M380.   16 rolls. DP.   16mm.

Index to Compiled Service Records of Confederate Soldiers who Served in Organizations From the State of North Carolina.
M230.   43 rolls. DP.   16mm.

Index to Compiled Service Records of Confederate Soldiers who Served in Organizations From the State of South Carolina.
M381.   35 rolls. DP.   16mm.

Index to Compiled Service Records of Confederate Soldiers who Served in Organizations From the State of Tennessee.
M231.   48 rolls. DP.   16mm.

Index to Compiled Service Records of Confederate Soldiers who Served in Organizations From the State of Texas.
M227.   41 rolls. DP.   16mm.

Index to Compiled Service Records of Confederate Soldiers who Served in Organizations From the State of Virginia.
M382.   62 rolls. DP.   16mm.

Compiled Service Records

Compiled Service Records of Confederate Soldiers who Served in Organizations Raised Directly by the Confederate Government.
M258.   123 rolls. DP.   16mm.

Compiled Service Records of Confederate Generals and Staff Officers, and Nonregimental Enlisted Men.
M331.   275 rolls. DP.   16mm.

Unfiled Papers and Slips Belonging in Confederate Compiled Service Records.
M347.   442 rolls. DP.   16mm.

Compiled Service Records of Confederate Soldiers who Served in Organizations From the State of Alabama.
M311.   508 rolls. DP.   16mm.

Compiled Service Records of Confederate Soldiers who Served in Organizations From the Territory of Arizona.
M318.   1 roll.   DP.   16mm.

Compiled Service Records of Confederate Soldiers who Served in Organizations From the State of Arkansas.
M317.   256 rolls. DP.   16mm.

Compiled Service Records of Confederate Soldiers who Served in Organizations From the State of Florida.
M251.   104 rolls. DP.   16mm.

Compiled Service Records of Confederate Soldiers who Served in Organizations From the State of Georgia.
M266.   607 rolls. DP.   16mm.

Compiled Service Records of Confederate Soldiers who Served in Organizations From the State of Kentucky.
M319.   136 rolls. DP.   16mm.

Compiled Service Records of Confederate Soldiers who Served in Organizations From the State of Louisiana.
M320.   414 rolls. DP.   16mm.

Compiled Service Records of Confederate Soldiers who Served in Organizations From the State of Maryland.
M321.   22 rolls.   DP.   16mm.

Compiled Service Records of Confederate Soldiers who Served in Organizations From the State of Mississippi.
M269.   427 rolls. DP.   16mm.

Compiled Service Records of Confederate Soldiers who Served in Organizations From the State of Missouri.
M322.   193 rolls. DP.   16mm.

Compiled Service Records of Confederate Soldiers who Served in Organizations From the State of North Carolina.
M270.   580 rolls. DP.   16mm.

Compiled Service Records of Confederate Soldiers who Served in Organizations From the State of South Carolina.
M267.   392 rolls. DP.   16mm.

Compiled Service Records of Confederate Soldiers who Served in Organizations From the State of Tennessee.
M268.   359 rolls. DP.   16mm.

Compiled Service Records of Confederate Soldiers who Served in Organizations From the State of Texas.
M323.   445 rolls. DP.   16mm.

Compiled Service Records of Confederate Soldiers who Served in Organizations From the State of Virginia.
M324.   1,075 rolls. DP.   16mm.

Other Records

Letters Sent by Lt. Col. G. H. Hill, Commander of the Confederate Ordnance Works at Tyler, Texas, 1864–1865.
M119.   1 roll.   DP.

Records Relating to Confederate Naval and Marine Personnel.
M260.   7 rolls.   DP.   16mm.

Union Provost Marshal's File of Papers Relating to Individual Civilians.
M345.   300 rolls. DP.   16mm.

Confederate Papers Relating to Citizens or Business Firms.
M346.   1,158 rolls.   DP.   16mm.

Records of the Louisiana State Government, 1850–1888, in the War Department Collection of Confederate Records.
M359.   24 rolls.   DP.

Index to the Letters Received by the Confederate Secretary of War, 1861–1865.
M409.   34 rolls.   DP.   16mm.

Index to the Letters Received by the Confederate Adjutant and Inspector General and by the Confederate Quartermaster General, 1861–1865.
M410.   41 rolls.   DP.   16mm.

Union Provost Marshal's File of Papers Relating to Two or More Civilians.
M416.   94 rolls.   DP.

Letters Received by the Confederate Secretary of War, 1861–1865.
M437. 151 rolls. DP.

Letters Received by the Confederate Quartermaster General, 1861–1865.
M469. 14 rolls. DP.

Letters Received by the Confederate Adjutant and Inspector General, 1861–1865.
M474. 164 rolls. DP.

Letters Sent by the Confederate Secretary of War, 1861–1865.
M522. 10 rolls. DP.

Letters Sent by the Confederate Secretary of War to the President, 1861–1865.
M523. 2 rolls. DP.

Telegrams Sent by the Confederate Secretary of War, 1861–1865.
M524. 1 roll. DP.

Selected Records of the War Department Relating to Confederate Prisoners of War, 1861–1865.
M598. 145 rolls. DP.

Telegrams Received by the Confederate Secretary of War, 1861–1865.
M618. 19 rolls. DP.

Letters and Telegrams Sent by the Confederate Adjutant and Inspector General, 1861–1865.
M627. 6 rolls.

Letters and Telegrams Sent by the Engineer Bureau of the Confederate War Department, 1861–1864.
M628. 5 rolls. DP.

Confederate States Army Casualties: Lists and Narrative Reports, 1861–1865.
M836. 7 rolls. DP.

Compiled Records Showing Service of Military Units in Confederate Organizations.
M861. 74 rolls. DP.

Letters and Telegrams Sent by the Confederate Quartermaster General, 1861–1865.
M900. 8 rolls. DP.

General Orders and Circulars of the Confederate War Department, 1861–1865.
M901. 1 roll. DP.

Papers Pertaining to Vessels of or Involved With the Confederate States of America: "Vessel Papers."
M909. 32 rolls. DP.

Orders and Circulars Issued by the Army of the Potomac and the Army and Department of Northern Virginia, C.S.A., 1861–1865.
M921. 4 rolls. DP.

Inspection Reports and Related Records Received by the Inspection Branch in the Confederate Adjutant and Inspector General's Office.
M935. 18 rolls. DP.

Records of the Virginia Forces, 1861.
M998. 7 rolls. DP.

➤Muster Rolls and Lists of Confederate Troops Paroled in North Carolina.
M1781. 7 rolls. DP.

Copies of Letters and Telegrams Received and Sent by Governor Zebulon B. Vance of North Carolina, 1862–1865.
T731. 1 roll.

Correspondence and Reports of the Confederate Treasury Department, 1861–1865.
T1025. 2 rolls.

Records of the Provost Marshal General's Bureau (Civil War). RG 110

Reports and Decisions of the Provost Marshal General, 1863–1866.
M621. 1 roll. DP.

Historical Reports of the State Acting Assistant Provost Marshal General and District Provost Marshals, 1865.
M1163. 5 rolls. DP.

Records of the Office of the Chief Signal Officer. RG 111

The Mathew B. Brady Collection of Civil War Photographs.
T252. 4 rolls.

Records of the Bureau of Reclamation. RG 115

Project Histories and Reports of Reclamation Bureau Projects, 1905–1925.
M96. 141 rolls.

Photographs of Irrigation Projects of the Bureau of Reclamation, 1902–1938.
M1145. 18 rolls.

Records of the American Expeditionary Forces (World War I), 1917–1923. RG 120

Records of the 27th Division of the American Expeditionary Forces (World War I), 1917–1919.
M819. 60 rolls. DP.

Records of the American Section of the Supreme War Council, 1917–1919.
M923. 21 rolls. DP.

Historical Files of the American Expeditionary Forces, North Russia, 1918–1919.
M924. 2 rolls. DP.

Cablegrams Exchanged Between General Headquarters, American Expeditionary Forces, and the War Department, 1917–1919.
M930. 19 rolls. DP.

Gorrell's History of the American Expeditionary Forces Air Service, 1917–1919.
M990. 58 rolls. DP.

Index to Correspondence of the Office of the Commander in Chief, American Expeditionary Forces, 1917–1919.
T900. 132 rolls. 16mm.

Letters Sent By The Superintendent of the United States Military Academy, 1838–1902.
M1039. 5 rolls. DP.

Records of the U.S. Court of Claims. RG 123

Eastern Cherokee Applications of the U.S. Court of Claims, 1906–1909.
M1104. 348 rolls. DP.

➤U.S. Court of Claims Docket Cards for Congressional Case Files, ca. 1884–ca. 1937.
M2007.   5 rolls.

Records of the Office of the Judge Advocate General (Navy). RG 125
Records of General Courts-Martial and Courts of Inquiry of the Navy Department, 1799–1867.
M273.   198 rolls. 16mm.

Records of the U.S. Marine Corps. RG 127
Muster Rolls of the U.S. Marine Corps, 1798–1860, 1866–1892.
T1118.   98 rolls.

Records of the Bureau of Prisons. RG 129
➤McNeil Island Penitentiary Records of Prisoners Received, 1887–1951.
M1619.   4 rolls.

Records of the Interstate Commerce Commission. RG 134
Annual Reports by Common Carriers to the Interstate Commerce Commission, 1888–1914.
T913.   1,348 rolls.   16mm.

Records of the Selective Service System, 1940–. RG 147
Method for Preservation of Selective Service Records, 1944–1945 (P.I. 27, Entry 56).
T1002.   2 rolls.

Records of Exposition, Anniversary, and Memorial Commissions. RG 148
Card Index to Pictures Collected by the George Washington Bicentennial Commission.
T271.   1 roll.

Records of the Office of the Judge Advocate General (Army). RG 153
See also RG 338 for World War II U.S. Army War Crimes Trial Records.

Proceedings of a Court of Inquiry Concerning the Conduct of Maj. Marcus A. Reno at the Battle of the Little Big Horn River on June 25 and 26, 1876.
M592.   2 rolls.

Investigation and Trial Papers Relating to the Assassination of President Lincoln.
M599.   16 rolls.   DP.

Registers of the Records of the Proceedings of the U.S. Army General Courts-Martial, 1809–1890.
M1105.   8 rolls.   DP.

➤United Nations War Crimes Commission List, 1944–1948.
M1536.   164 cards (microfiche).

➤Col. Charles L. Decker's Collection of Records Relating to Military Justice and the Revision of Military Law, 1948–1956.
M1739.   31 rolls.   DP.

Records Relating to the Army Career of Henry Ossian Flipper, 1873–1882.
T1027.   1 roll.

General Court Martial of Gen. George Armstrong Custer, 1867.
T1103.   1 roll.

Records of the Wage and Hour Division. RG 155
Wage Data on Wage and Hour Cases, Region 5, 1938–1944.
T950.   9 rolls.

Records of the Office of the Inspector General (Army). RG 159
Inspection Reports of the Office of the Inspector General, 1814–1842.
M624.   3 rolls.   DP.

Records of the Federal Works Agency. RG 162
Checklist of Historical Records Survey Publications, Apr. 1943.
T1028.   1 roll.

Records of the War Department General and Special Staffs. RG 165
Indexes to Records of the War College Division and Related General Staff Offices, 1903–1919.
M912.   49 rolls.   DP.

Papers and Minutes of Meetings of Principal World War II Allied Military Conferences, 1941–1945.
M995.   4 rolls.   DP.

Record Cards to the Correspondence of the War College Division, Related General Staff, and Adjutant General Offices, 1902–1919.
M1023.   37 rolls.   DP.

Name and Subject Index to the General Correspondence of the War Plans Division, 1921–1942.
M1080.   18 rolls.   DP.

Name Index to Correspondence of the Military Intelligence Division of the War Department Staff, 1917–1941.
M1194.   262 rolls. DP.

Correspondence of the Military Intelligence Division Relating to General, Political, Economic, and Military Conditions in Japan, 1918–1941.
M1216.   31 rolls.   DP.

Registers of Communication Received From Military Attaches and Other Intelligence Officers ("Dispatch Lists"), 1889–1941.
M1271.   5 rolls.   DP.

Correspondence of the Military Intelligence Division Correspondence Relating to "Negro Subversion," 1917–1941.
M1440.   6 rolls.   DP.

Correspondence of the Military Intelligence Division Relating to General, Political, Economic, and Military Conditions in Russia and the Soviet Union, 1918–1941.
M1443.   23 rolls.   DP.

Correspondence of the Military Intelligence Division Relating to General, Political, Economic, and Military Conditions in China, 1918–41.
M1444.   19 rolls.   DP.

Correspondence of the Military Intelligence Division Relating to General, Political, Economic, and Military Conditions in Spain, 1918–1941.
M1445.   12 rolls.   DP.

Correspondence and Record Cards of the Military Intelligence Division Relating to General, Political, Economic, and Military Conditions in Italy, 1918–1941.
M1446.   26 rolls.   DP.

Geographic Index to Correspondence of the Military Intelligence Division of the War Department General Staff, 1917–41.
M1474.   17 rolls.   DP.

Correspondence and Record Cards of the Military Intelligence Division Relating to General, Political, and Military Conditions in Central America, 1918–1941.
M1488.   12 rolls.   DP.

Correspondence of the Military Intelligence Division Relating to General, Political, and Military Conditions in Scandanavia and Finland, 1918–1941.
M1497.   12 rolls.   DP.

Correspondence and Record Cards of the Military Intelligence Division Relating to General, Political, Economic, and Military Conditions in Cuba and the West Indies, 1918–1941.
M1507.   10 rolls.   DP.

Correspondence and Record Cards of the Military Intelligence Division Relating to General, Political, Economic, and Military Conditions in Poland and the Baltic States, 1918–1941.
M1508.   10 rolls.   DP.

►The Military Intelligence Division Regional File Relating to China, 1922–1944.
M1513.   58 rolls.   DP.

List of Photographs and Photographic Negatives Relating to the War for the Union (War Department Subject Catalogue No. 5, 1897).
T251.   1 roll.

General Records of the Department of Labor. RG 174

Reports of the U.S. Commission on Industrial Relations, 1912–1915.
T4.   15 rolls.

Records of the War Production Board. RG 179

Press Releases of the Advisory Commission to the Council of National Defense, June 3, 1940–Jan. 15, 1941.
M185.   1 roll.   DP.

Progress Reports of the Advisory Commission to the Council of National Defense, July 24, 1940–May 28, 1941.
M186.   1 roll.   DP.

Numbered Document File of the Advisory Commission to the Council of National Defense, 1904–1941.
M187.   2 rolls.   DP.

Numbered Document File of the Council of the Office of Production Management, 1940–1942.
M195.   1 roll.   DP.

Numbered Document File of the Supply Priorities and Allocations Board, Sept. 2, 1941–Jan. 15, 1942.
M196.   1 roll.   DP.

Index to the War Production Board Policy Documentation File, 1939–1947.
M911   86 rolls.   DP.

Applications for Certificates of Necessity, 1941–1945.
M1200.   1,095 rolls.

War Production Board Press Releases and Indexes, 1940–1947.
M1239.   53 rolls.

Records of Naval Districts and Shore Establishments. RG 181

Activity Location Cards of the Fleet Post Office, San Francisco, California, 1940–1945.
T1015.   2 rolls.

Historical Records of the Newport Naval Training Station Rhode Island, 1883–1948.
T1017.   1 roll.

Records of Spanish Governors of Puerto Rico. RG 186

Expediente sobre la rebelion de Lares, 1868–1869 (Case File on the Rebellion of Lares).
T1120.   6 rolls.

Registro central de esclavos, 1872 (Slave Schedules).
T1121.   8 rolls.

Reales ordenes, 1792–1793, y reales ordenes y decretos, 1767–1854 (Royal Orders and Decrees).
T1122.   1 roll.

Extranjeros (Foreigners) in Puerto Rico, 1872–1880.
T1170.   19 rolls.

Records of the National Resources Planning Board. RG 187

Reports of the National Resources Planning Board, 1936–1943.
M120.   5 rolls.   DP.

Records of the Office of Price Administration. RG 188

Studies and Reports of the Office of Price Administration, 1941–1946.
M164.   2 rolls.

Records of the War Relocation Authority. RG 210

Community Analysis Reports and Community Analysis Trend Reports of the War Relocation Authority, 1942–1946.
M1342.   29 rolls.   DP.

Records of the Accounting Officers of the Department of the Treasury. RG 217

Miscellaneous Treasury Accounts of the First Auditor (Formerly the Auditor) of the Treasury Department, September 6, 1790–1840.
M235.   1,170 rolls.

Letters Sent by the Commissioner of Customs Relating to Smuggling, 1865–1869.
M497.   1 roll.

Letters Sent by the Commissioner of Customs Relating to Captured and Abandoned Property, 1868–1875.
M498.   1 roll.

Records of the Board of Commissioners for the Emancipation of Slaves in the District of Columbia, 1862–1863.
M520.   6 rolls.   DP.

➤Southern Claims Commission Approved Claims, 1871–1880: Georgia.
M1658.   761 cards   DP.
          (microfiche).

➤Claims for Georgia Militia Campaigns Against Indians on the Frontier, 1792–1827.
M1745.   5 rolls.   DP.

➤Final Revolutionary War Pension Payment Vouchers: Georgia
M1746.   6 rolls.   DP.

Selected Records of the General Accounting Office Relating to the Fremont Expeditions and the California Battalion, 1818–1890.
T135.   3 rolls.

Civil War Direct Tax Assessment Lists: Tennessee.
T227.   6 rolls.

Ledgers of Payments, 1818–1872, to U.S. Pensioners Under Acts of 1818 Through 1858, From Records of the Office of the Third Auditor of the Treasury.
T718.   23 rolls.

Day Book of the Register's Office of the Treasury, 1789–1791.
T964.   1 roll.

Register of Audits of "Miscellaneous Treasury Accounts" (First Auditor's Office).
T899.   1 roll.

Records of the U.S. Joint Chiefs of Staff. RG 218

German and Japanese Surrender Documents of World War II and the Korean Armistice Agreements.
T826.   1 roll.

Capt. Tracy B. Kittredge's
The Evolution of Global Strategy.
T1174.   1 roll.

Records of Temporary Committees, Commissions, and Boards. RG 220

Public Hearings of the Commission on Wartime Relocation and Internment of Civilians.
M1293.   6 rolls.

Challenger Commission P.C. Numbered Documents, 1986.
M1496.   73 rolls.   16mm.

Indexes to Records of the Presidential Commission on the Space Shuttle *Challenger* Accident, 1986.
M1501.   30 cards (microfiche).

Records of Joint Army and Navy Boards and Committees. RG 225.

Records of the Joint Board, 1903–1947.
M1421.   21 rolls.   DP.

Records of the Office of Strategic Services. RG 226

➤Records of the Research and Analysis Branch, Office of Strategic Services ("Regular" Series), 1941–1945.
M1499.   389 rolls.

➤History of the London Office of the OSS.
M1623.   10 rolls.   DP.

➤Records of the Office of Strategic Services, Washington Director's Office Administrative Files, 1941–1945.
M1642.   136 rolls.

➤Strategic Services Unit Intelligence Reports, 1945–1946.
M1656.   5 rolls.

➤The Boston Series, 1941–1945 (Intelligence Files, Office of the Director, OSS).
M1740.   3 rolls.

Records of the Office of Scientific Research and Development. RG 227

➤Bush-Conant File Relating to the Development of the Atomic Bomb, 1940–1945.
M1392.   14 rolls.   DP.

Reports of the Office of Scientific Research and Development, 1941–1947.
T1012.   487 rolls.

Records of the U.S. House of Representatives. RG 233

➤Journals of the U.S. House of Representatives, 1789–1817.
M1264.   17 rolls.   DP.

➤Bill Books of the U.S. House of Representatives, 1814–1817.
M1265.   1 roll.   DP.

➤Petition Books of the U.S. House of Representatives, 1789–1817.
M1266.   2 rolls.   DP.

➤Transcribed Reports of the Committees of the U.S. House of Representatives, 1789–1841.
M1267.   15 rolls.   DP.

➤Transcribed Reports and Communications Transmitted by the Executive Branch to the U.S. House of Representatives, 1789–1819.
M1268.   15 rolls.   DP.

Barred and Disallowed Case Files of the Southern Claims Commission, 1871–1880.
M1407.   4,829 cards   DP.
          (microfiche).

Hearings of the House Select Committee That Investigated the Race Riots in East St. Louis in 1917.
M1167.   7 rolls.   DP.

➤Unbound Records of the U.S. House of Representatives, Fifth Congress, 1797–1799.
M1705.   1 roll.   DP.

➤Unbound Records of the U.S. House of Representatives, Sixth Congress, 1799–1801.
M1707.   4 rolls.   DP.

Unbound Records of the House of Representatives for the Eighth Congress, 1803–1805.
M1404. 5 rolls. DP.

Records of the Reconstruction Finance Corporation. RG 234

➤Minutes of the Defense Plant Corporation, 1940–1945.
M1637. 105 rolls.

German Reports on Synthetic Rubber, 1937–1945.
T948. 13 rolls.

Agreements and Subject Files of the Office of Synthetic Rubber, 1941–1953.
T949. 41 rolls. 16mm.

National Archives Collection of World War II War Crimes Records. RG 238

U.S. Nuernberg War Crimes Trials

See also RG 338, Records of the United States Army Commands, 1942–, under Department of the Army.

Records of the U.S. Nuernberg War Crimes Trials: *United States of America* v. *Karl Brandt et al.* (Case I), Nov. 21, 1946–Aug. 20, 1947.
M887. 46 rolls. DP.

Records of the U.S. Nuernberg War Crimes Trials: *United States of America* v. *Erhard Milch* (Case II), Nov. 13, 1946–Apr. 17, 1947.
M888. 13 rolls. DP.

Records of the U.S. Nuernberg War Crimes Trials: *United States of America* v. *Josef Altstoetter et al.* (Case III), Feb. 17–Dec. 4, 1947.
M889. 53 rolls. DP.

Records of the U.S. Nuernberg War Crimes Trials: *United States of America* v. *Oswald Pohl et al.* (Case IV), Jan. 13, 1947–Aug. 11, 1948.
M890. 38 rolls. DP.

Records of the U.S. Nuernberg War Crimes Trials: *United States of America* v. *Friedrich Flick et al.* (Case V), Mar. 3–Dec. 22, 1947.
M891. 42 rolls. DP.

Records of the U.S. Nuernberg War Crimes Trials: *United States of America* v. *Carl Krauch et al.* (Case VI), Aug. 14, 1947–July 30, 1948.
M892. 113 rolls. DP.

Records of the U.S. Nuernberg War Crimes Trials: *United States of America* v. *Wilhelm List et al.* (Case VII), July 8, 1947–Feb. 19, 1948.
M893. 48 rolls. DP.

Records of the U.S. Nuernberg War Crimes Trials: *United States of America* v. *Ulrich Greifelt et al.* (Case VIII), Oct. 10, 1947–Mar. 10, 1948.
M894. 38 rolls. DP.

Records of the U.S. Nuernberg War Crimes Trials: *United States of America* v. *Otto Ohlendorf et al.* (Case IX), Sept. 15, 1947–Apr. 10, 1948.
M895. 38 rolls. DP.

Records of the U.S. Nuernberg War Crimes Trials: *United States of America* v. *Alfried Krupp et al.* (Case X), Aug. 16, 1947–July 31, 1948.
M896. 69 rolls. DP.

Records of the U.S. Nuernberg War Crimes Trials *United States of America* v. *Ernst von Weizsaecker et al.* (Case XI), Dec. 20, 1947–Apr. 14, 1949.
M897. 173 rolls. DP.

Records of the U.S. Nuernberg War Crimes Trials: *United States of America* v. *Wilhelm von Leeb et al.* (Case XII), Nov. 28, 1947–Oct. 28, 1948.
M898. 69 rolls. DP.

Records of the U.S. Nuernberg War Crimes Trials: NM Series, 1874–1946.
M936. 1 roll. DP.

Records of the U.S. Nuernberg War Crimes Trials: NP Series, 1934–1946.
M942. 1 roll. DP.

Records of the U.S. Nuernberg War Crimes Trials: WA Series, 1940–1945.
M946. 1 roll. DP.

Records of the U.S. Nuernberg War Crimes Trials: Guertner Diaries, Oct. 5, 1934–Dec. 24, 1938.
M978. 3 rolls. DP.

Records of the U.S. Nuernberg War Crimes Trials: Interrogations, 1946–1949.
M1019. 91 rolls. DP.

Interrogation Records Prepared for War Crimes Proceedings at Nuernberg, 1945–1947.
M1270. 31 rolls. DP.

Nuernberg Trials Records: Register Cards to the NG Document Series, 1946–1949.
M1278. 3 rolls. DP.

Nuernberg Trials Records: Register Cards to the NOKW Document Series, 1946–1949.
M1291. 2 rolls. DP.

Nuernberg Trials Records: Register Cards to the NI Document Series, 1946–1949.
M1397. 8 rolls. DP.

Records of the U.S. Nuernberg War Crimes Trials: NOKW Series.
T1119. 47 rolls.

Records of the U.S. Nuernberg War Crimes Trials: NG Series, 1933–1948.
T1139. 70 rolls.

Records of the U.S. Nuernberg War Crimes Trials: NI Series, 1933–1948.
T301. 164 rolls.

Other World War II Crimes Records

Court Papers, Journal, Exhibits, and Judgments of the International Military Tribunal for the Far East, 1900–1948.
T918. 61 rolls.

Prosecution Exhibits Submitted to the International Military Tribunal.
T988. 54 rolls.

War Diaries and Correspondence of Gen. Alfred Jodl.
T989. 2 rolls.

Mauthausen Death Books.
T990. 2 rolls.

U.S. Trial Brief and Document Books.
T991. 1 roll.

Diary of Hans Frank.
T992. 12 rolls. 16mm.

Records of the Patent and Trademark Office. RG 241

Patent Drawings, 1792–1833.
T280.   2 rolls.

➤Patent Drawings, 1791–1877.
T1239.   320 rolls.

National Archives Collection of Foreign Records Seized, 1941–. RG 242

An Exhibit of German Military Documents From the Heeresarchiv Potsdam, 1679–1935.
M129.   2 rolls.

Papers of Gen. Hans von Seeckt, 1866–1936.
M132.   28 rolls.

Papers of Gen. Wilhelm Groener, 1867–1939.
M137.   27 rolls.

Papers of Herman von Boyen, ca. 1787–1849.
M207.   12 rolls.

Papers of August von Gneisenau, ca. 1785–1831.
M211.   43 rolls.

Papers of Hans Karl von Winterfeldt, 1707–1757.
M953.   2 rolls.

Papers of August Wilhelm Herzog von Braunschweig-Bevern, 1717–1781.
M954.   1 roll.

Papers of Friedrich Wilhelm III of Prussia, 1770–1840.
M955.   1 roll.

Papers of Albrecht Graf von Roon, 1803–1879.
M956.   2 rolls.

Papers of Lieutenant General Heinrich Scheüch, 1864–1946.
M957.   1 roll.

Papers of Christoph Emanuel Hermann Ritter Mertz von Quirnheim, 1866–1947.
M958.   2 rolls.

Papers of Gerhard Johann David von Scharnhorst, 1775–1813.
M959.   12 rolls.

Papers of Graf Helmuth Carl Bernhard von Moltke, 1800–1891.
M960.   6 rolls.

Papers of Alfred Graf von Schlieffen, 1833–1913.
M961.   8 rolls.

Prussian Mobilization Records, 1866–1918.
M962.   5 rolls.

Records of the Royal Bavarian War Ministry and Other Bavarian Military Authorities, 1866–1913.
M963.   7 rolls.

➤Guide to the Records of the German Navy, 1850–1945.
M1743.   1 roll.

Records of the Reich Ministry for Public Enlightenment and Propaganda, 1936–1944.
T70.   133 rolls.

Records of the Reich Ministry of Economics.
T71.   149 rolls.

Records of the Reich Ministry for Armaments and War Production.
T73.   193 rolls.

Records of the Office of the Reich Commissioner for the Strengthening of Germandom.
T74.   20 rolls.

Records of the Office of the Deputy for Serbian Economy.
T75.   89 rolls.

Records of the Todt Organization.
T76.   7 rolls.

Records of the Headquarters of the German Armed Forces High Command.
T77.   1,581 rolls.

Records of the Headquarters of the German Army High Command.
T78.   704 rolls.

Records of German Army Areas.
T79.   315 rolls.

Records of the National Socialist German Labor Party.
T81.   732 rolls.

Records of Nazi Cultural and Research Institutions.
T82.   549 rolls.

Records of Private Austrian, Dutch, and German Enterprises.
T83.   248 rolls.

Miscellaneous German Records Collection.
T84.   440 rolls.

Records of the All-Union (Russian) Communist Party (Smolensk Archives), 1917–1941.
T87.   69 rolls.

Miscellaneous Russian Records Collection.
T88.   4 rolls.

Records of the German Foreign Office Received by the Department of State.
T120.   5,055 rolls.

Records of the German Foreign Office Received by the Department of State From St. Antony's College.
T136.   144 rolls.

Records of the German Foreign Office Received by the Department of State From the University of California (Project I).
T139.   445 rolls.

German Foreign Ministry Archives, 1867–1920, Filmed by the American Historical Association.
T149.   434 rolls.

Records of the Reich Leader of the SS and Chief of the German Police.
T175.   678 rolls.

Data Sheets to Microfilmed Captured German Records.
T176.   34 rolls.

Records of the Reich Air Ministry (Reichsluftfahrtministerium).
T177.   52 rolls.

Fragmentary Records of Miscellaneous Reich Ministries and Offices, 1919–1945.
T178.   28 rolls.

Records of German and Japanese Embassies and Consulates, 1890–1945.
T179.   78 rolls.

Records of Private Individuals (Captured German Records).
T253.   62 rolls.

Records of the German Foreign Office Received by the Department of State From the British Museum.
T264.   2 rolls.

German Military and Technical
Manuals, 1910–1945.
T283. 162 rolls.

Archives of the German Embassy at
Washington (American Historical
Association Project I).
T290. 52 rolls.

Papers of German Diplomats
(Nachlasse and Asservate),
1833–1927 (American Historical
Association Project II).
T291. 25 rolls.

Records of German Field Commands:
Army Groups.
T311. 304 rolls.

Records of German Field Commands:
Armies.
T312. 1,696 rolls.

Records of German Field Commands:
Panzer Armies.
T313. 489 rolls.

Records of German Field Commands:
Corps.
T314. 1,670 rolls.

Records of German Field Commands:
Divisions.
T315. 3,256 rolls.

Records of the Headquarters of
the German Air Force High
Command (Oberkommando der
Luftwaffe-OKL).
T321. 274 rolls.

A Catalog of Files and Microfilms of
the German Foreign Ministry Archives,
1867–1920.
T322. 1 roll.

Miscellaneous SS Records—The
Einwandererzentralstelle Waffen-SS,
and SS Oberabschnitte.
T354. 799 rolls.

Name Index of Jews Whose
German Nationality Was Annulled
by the Nazi Regime (Berlin
Documents Center).
T355. 9 rolls.

Reich Office for Soil Exploration
(Reichsamt fur Bodenforschung).
T401. 7 rolls.

German Air Force Reports:
Luftgaukommandos, Flak, Deutsche
Luftwaffenmission in Rumenien.
T405. 64 rolls.

*Index of Microfilmed Records of the
German Foreign Ministry and the
Reich's Chancellery Covering the
Weimar Period.*
T407. 1 roll.

Records of the Reich Ministry for the
Occupied Eastern Territories, 1941–
1945 (Reichsministerium fur die
besetzten Ostgebiete).
T454. 107 rolls.

Documents Concerning Jews in the
Berlin Document Center.
T457. 14 rolls. 16mm and 35mm.

Records of the Reich Commissioner for
the Baltic States (Reichskommissar fur
das Ostland), 1941–1945.
T459. 45 rolls.

Records of German Field Commands:
Rear Areas, Occupied Territories, and
Others.
T501. 363 rolls.

Captured German Records Filmed at
Berlin (American Historical
Association), 1960.
T580. 986 rolls.

Personal Papers of Benito Mussolini.
Also, Some Official Records of the
Italian Foreign Office and the Ministry
of Culture, 1922–1944.
T586. 318 rolls.

Records of the Headquarters of the
German Navy High Command (OKM).
T608. 8 rolls.

Captured German Documents Filmed
at Berlin (University of Nebraska).
T611. 49 rolls.

Papers of Count Ciano (Lisbon Papers)
Received From the Department of State.
T816. 3 rolls.

Collection of Italian Military Records,
1935–1943.
T821. 506 rolls.

The Von Rhoden Collection of
Research Materials on the Role of the
German
Air Force in World War II, 1911–1947.
T971. 73 rolls.

Collection of Correspondence of
Herbert von Bismarck, 1881–1883.
T972. 1 roll.

Collection of Hungarian Political and
Military Records, 1909–1945.
T973. 21 rolls.

Records of the Economic Enterprises
of the SS (Econombetriebe, SS
Wirtschafts-Verwaltungshauptamt),
1936–1945.
T976. 37 rolls.

Records of the German Navy, 1850–
1945, Received From the United
States Naval History Division.
T1022. 4,225 rolls.

Records of the German Foreign Office
Filmed for the University of London.
T1026. 25 rolls.

Records of the German Foreign Ministry
Pertaining to China, 1919–1935.
T1141. 31 rolls.

Transcript of *Cossman* v. *Gruber*
(Dolchstoss-Prozess), Munich,
Oct. 19–Nov. 17, 1925.
T1173. 2 rolls.

Records of the U.S. Strategic Bombing Survey. RG 243

Final Reports of the U.S. Strategic
Bombing Survey, 1945–1947.
M1013. 25 rolls. DP.

Tactical Mission Reports of the 20th
and 21st Bomber Commands, 1945.
M1159. 6 rolls.

Joint Army-Navy Intelligence Studies
(JANIS), 1944–1945.
M1169. 20 rolls.3.

Japanese Resources Reference
Notebooks, 1945–1947.
M1199. 6 rolls.

►Statistical Reports Covering Allied and
U.S. Air Force Attack Data, 1945–1946.
M1205. 11 rolls.

►Twentieth Air Force Damage
Assessment Cards, 1945.
M1651. 1 roll.

►U.S. Strategic Bombing Survey
(Pacific): Intelligence Library, 1932–47.
M1652. 118 rolls.

►Japanese Air Target Analyses,
Objective Folders, and Aerial
Photographs, 1942–1945.
M1653. 7 rolls.

►Interrogation of Japanese Leaders
and Responses to Questionnaires,
1945–1946.
M1654. 9 rolls.

➤U.S. Strategic Bombing Survey (Pacific): Reports and Other Records, 1928–1947.
M1655.   507 rolls.

➤Land-Based Navy and Marine Corps Aircraft Action Reports, 1944–1945.
M1720.   36 rolls.

➤Damage Assessment Reports, 1945.
M1721.   17 rolls.

➤Miscellaneous Documents Relating to the Atomic Bombing of Japan, Allied and Japanese Military Operations in the Pacific, and Japanese Reports on the Chinese Communist Party.
M1738.   8 rolls.

Records of the Commissary General of Prisoners. RG 249.
➤Selected Records of the War Department Commissary General of Prisoners Relating to Federal Prisoners of War Confined at Andersonville, Georgia, 1864–1865.
M1303.   6 rolls.   DP.

Records of the American Commisssion to Negotiate Peace. RG 256
General Records of the American Commission to Negotiate Peace, 1918–1931.
M820.   563 rolls. DP.

"Inquiry Documents" (Special Reports and Studies), 1917–1919.
M1107.   47 rolls.

Records of United States Occupation Headquarters, World War II. RG 260
Minutes of the Division Staff Meetings of the U.S. Group Council for Germany and the Office of Military Government for Germany (U.S.) (OMGUS), Nov. 1944–Aug. 1949.
M1075.   4 rolls.   DP.

Records of Former Russian Agencies. RG 261
Records of the Russian-American Company, 1802–1867.
M11.   77 rolls.   DP.

➤Records of the Imperial Russian Consulates in the United States, 1862–1922.
M1486.   180 rolls. DP.

➤Records of Imperial Russian Consulates in Canada, 1898–1922.
M1742.   83 rolls.   DP.

Records of the Central Intelligence Agency. RG 263
➤Records of the Shanghai Municipal Police, 1894–1949.
M1750.   1 roll.

Records of the Supreme Court of the United States. RG 267
The Revolutionary War Prize Cases: Records of the Court of Appeal in Cases of Capture, 1776–1787.
M162.   15 rolls.   DP.

Appellate Case Files of the U.S. Supreme Court, 1792–1831.
M214.   96 rolls.   DP.

Minutes of the U.S. Supreme Court, 1790–1950.
M215.   41 rolls.   DP.

Dockets of the U.S. Supreme Court, 1791–1950.
M216.   27 rolls.   DP.

Attorney Rolls of the U.S. Supreme Court, 1790–1951.
M217.   4 rolls.   DP.

Index to Appellate Case Files of the U.S. Supreme Court, 1792–1909.
M408.   20 rolls.   DP.   l6mm.

Original Opinions of the Justices of the U.S. Supreme Court Delivered at the January Term 1832; and Opinions and Other Case Papers of Chief Justice Marshall, 1834 and 1835 Terms.
T57.   1 roll.

Records of the President's Commission on the Assassination of President Kennedy. RG 272
Numbered Documents of the President's Commission on the Assassination of President Kennedy.
M1124.   42 rolls.   DP.

"Key Persons" Files of the President's Commission on the Assassination of President Kennedy, 1963–1964.
M1289.   34 rolls.

"Other Individuals and Organizations" File of the President's Commission on the Assassination of President Kennedy, 1963–1964.
M1402.   39 rolls.   DP.

➤Report and Hearings of the President's Commission on the Assassination of President Kennedy.
M1758.   11 rolls.

Records of the National Security Council. RG 273
➤National Security Council Policy Papers, 1947–1961.
M1534.   322 cards   DP.
        (microfiche).

Records of the Government of American Samoa. RG 284
Records of the Government of American Samoa, 1900–1958.
T1182.   62 rolls.

Publications of the United States Government. RG 287
The *Stars and Stripes*: Newspaper of the U.S. Armed Forces in Europe, the Mediterranean, and North Africa, 1942–1964.
M1506.   138 rolls. DP.

➤*Stars and Stripes*: Newspaper of the U.S. Armed Forces in the Pacific, 1945–1963.
M1624.   166 rolls. DP.

➤Indexes and Lists to Army Technical and Administrative Publications, 1940–1979.
M1641.   29 rolls.   DP.

Records of the Office of Price Stabilization. RG 295

Defense History Program Studies Prepared During the Korean War Period.
T460.   3 rolls.

Records of the U.S. Information Agency. RG 306

New York Times Paris Bureau Photographs, 1900–1940 (A Series).
M1149.   1 roll.

New York Times Paris Bureau Photographs, 1900–1940 (B Series).
M1150.   2 rolls.

New York Times Paris Bureau Photographs, 1900–1940 (Letterless Series).
M1151.   95 rolls.

New York Times Paris Bureau Photographs, 1900–1940 (C Series).
M1152.   28 rolls.

New York Times Paris Bureau Photographs, 1924–1940 (D Series).
M1153   7 rolls.

New York Times Paris Bureau Photographs, 1940–1945 (E Series).
M1154.   1 roll.

New York Times Paris Bureau Photographs, 1945–1950 (V Series).
M1155.   33 rolls.

Records of Allied Operational and Occupation Headquarters, World War II. RG 331

Reviews of the Yokohama Class B and Class C War Crimes Trials by the 8th Army Judge Advocate, 1946–1949.
M1112.   5 rolls.   DP.

Subject File Headings for the Records of the Allied Control Commission (Italy), 1943–1947.
M1190.   5 rolls.   DP.

➤Copies of Judgments of the International Military Tribunal for the Far East, 1948.
M1660.   7 rolls.

➤Transcripts from the Case of the *United States of America v. Soemu Toyoda and Hiroshi Tamura*, 1946–1948.
M1661.   4 rolls.

➤Studies, Reports, and Other Reference Documents of the Allied Operational and Occupation Headquarters, World War II, Supreme Commander Allied Powers, International Prosecution Section, 1944–1948.
M1662.   44 rolls.

➤International Prosecution Section Staff: Historical Files Relating to Cases Tried Before the International Military Tribunal for the Far East, 1945–1948.
M1663.   66 rolls.

➤Miscellaneous Records of the Allied Operational and Occupation Headquarters, World War II, Supreme Commander Allied Powers, International Prosecution Section, 1945–1948.
M1664.   9 rolls.

➤Prosecution and Defense Summations for Cases Tried Before International Military Tribunal for the Far East, 1948.
M1665.   21 rolls.

➤Narrative Summary and Transcripts of Court Proceedings for Cases Tried Before the International Military Tribunal for the Far East, 1946–1948.
M1666.   64 rolls.

➤Transcripts of Proceedings in Chambers for Cases Tried Before the International Military Tribunal for the Far East, 1946–1948.
M1667.   I roll.

➤Records of the Chief Prosecutor Relating to Preparation for and Conduct of Cases Tried by the International Prosecution Section Before the International Military Tribunal for the Far East, 1946–1948.
M1668.   18 rolls.

➤Records of the International Prosecution Section: Prosecution's Opening Statements, Summary of Evidence, and Copies of Indictments, 1946.
M1669.   2 rolls.

➤War Crimes Trial Documents Collected by the International Prosecution Section for Use Before the International Military Tribunal for the Far East, 1945–1947.
M1679.   1 roll.

➤Documents Assembled by the International Prosecution Section for Use as Exhibits Before the International Military Tribunal for the Far East, 1945–1947.
M1680.   34 rolls.

➤Reports, Orders, Studies, and Other Background Documents Gathered by the International Prosecution Section, 1945–1947.
M1681.   9 rolls.

➤Indexes to Numerical Case Files Relating to Particular Incidents and Suspected War Criminals, International Prosecution Section, 1945–1947.
M1682.   4 rolls.

➤Numerical Case Files Relating to Particular Incidents and Suspected War Criminals, International Prosecution Section, 1945–1947.
M1683.   73 rolls.

➤International Prosecution Section Documents Relating to Witnesses for the Prosecution and the Defense, 1946–1947.
M1684.   21 rolls.

➤Indexes of Exhibits of the Prosecution and of the Defense, Introduced as Evidence Before the International Military Tribunal for the Far East, 1945–1947.
M1685.   2 rolls.

➤Exhibits of the Prosecution and of the Defense Introduced as Evidence Before the International Military Tribunal for the Far East, 1945–1947.
M1686.   17 rolls.

➤Index to Court Exhibits in English and Japanese, International Prosecution Section, 1945–1947.
M1687.   I roll.

➤Court Exhibits in English and Japanese, International Prosecution Section, 1945–1947.
M1688.   48 rolls.

➤Indexes to Numerical Evidentiary Documents Assembled by the Prosecution for Use as Evidence Before the International Military Tribunal for the Far East, 1945–1947.
M1689.   8 rolls.

➤Numerical Evidentiary Documents Assembled as Evidence by the Prosecution for Use Before the International Military Tribunal for the Far East, 1945–1947.
M1690.   477 rolls.

➤Indexes to Documents Presented as Evidence by the Defense and Defense Documents Rejected as Evidence Before the International Military Tribunal for the Far East, 1945–1947.
M1691.   2 rolls.

➤Documents Presented as Evidence by the Defense Before the International Military Tribunal for the Far East, 1945–1947.
M1692.   19 rolls.

➤Defense Documents Rejected as Evidence Before the International Military Tribunal for the Far East, 1946–1947.
M1693.   16 rolls.

➤Alphabetical Series of Defense Documents Presented for Evidence and Rejected by the International Military Tribunal for the Far East, 1945–1947.
M1694.   3 rolls.

➤Index to Names of Witnesses and Suspected War Crimes Perpetrators Who Appeared Before the International Military Tribunal for the Far East, 1945–1947.
M1695.   1 roll.

➤Indexes to Files Showing the Receipt and Distribution of Defense Documents and the Receipt of Affidavits from Prisoners of War and Other Sources, 1946–1948.
M1696.   2 rolls.

➤Analyses of the Documentary Evidence Introduced by the Prosecution Before the International Military Tribunal for the Far East, 1946–1948.
M1697.   6 rolls.

➤Indexes to Court Documents Including Orders, Rules of Procedure, and Copies of the Indictment and Motions of the Defense, 1946–1948.
M1698.   1 roll.

➤Court Documents Including Orders, Rules of Procedure, and Copies of the Indictment and Motions of the Defense, 1946–1948.
M1699.   3 rolls.

➤Indexes and Lists of Witnesses for the Defense and for the Prosecution Before the International Military Tribunal for the Far East, 1946–1948.
M1700.   1 roll.

➤Numeric Records of the Prosecution Attorneys Relating to the Prosecution's Evidence Before the International Military Tribunal for the Far East, 1946–1948.
M1701.   4 rolls.

➤Records Pertaining to Rules and Procedures Governing the Conduct of Japanese War Crimes Trials, Atrocities Committed Against Chinese Laborers, and Background Investigations of Major Japanese War Criminals.
M1722.   17 rolls.

➤Miscellaneous Documents Relating to Japan's Economic, Industrial, Military, and Diplomatic Activities Used as Background Materials by the International Prosecution Section, 1929–1945.
M1723.   7 rolls.

➤Nuremberg Transcripts Used as Reference Documents by the International Prosecution Section for the International Military Tribunal for the Far East, 1945–1947.
M1724.   8 rolls.

➤Supreme Commander for the Allied Powers: Report on the Summation of U.S. Army Military and Non-Military Activities in the Far East, 1945–1947.
M1725.   3 rolls.

➤Records of Trials and Clemency Petitions for Accused Japanese War Criminals Tried at Yokohama, Japan, by a Military Commission Appointed by the Commanding General, Eighth Army, 1946–1948.
M1726.   59 rolls.

➤Records of Trials of Accused Japanese War Criminals Tried at Manila, Philippines, by a Military Commission Convened by the Commanding General of the United States Army in the Western Pacific, 1945–1947.
M1727.   34 rolls.

➤Records of the Trial of Accused War Criminal Hiroshi Tamura, Tried by a Military Tribunal Appointed by the Supreme Commander of the Allied Powers, Tokyo, Japan, 1948–1949.
M1728.   3 rolls.

➤Records of the Trial of Accused War Criminal Soemu Toyoda, Tried by a Military Tribunal Appointed by the Supreme Commander of the Allied Powers, Tokyo, Japan, 1948–1949.
M1729.   7 rolls.

➤Miscellaneous Documents Relating to the Japanese Attack on Pearl Harbor and Other Japanese Military Activities, 1941–1945.
M1730.   1 roll.

➤Photostatic Copies of Newspaper Articles Relating to Japanese War Crimes and War Crimes Trials, 1943–1948.
M1731.   1 roll.

➤Miscellaneous International Prosecution Documents Used as Background in Preparation for the International Military Tribunal for the Far East, 1940–1948.
M1732.   19 rolls.

➤Photographs of Japanese Soldiers and of Allied Prisoners of War, 1942–1945.
M1733.   1 roll.

Records of U.S. Theaters of War, World War II.
RG 332

"Eyes Alone" Correspondence of General Joseph W. Stilwell, January 1942–October 1944.
M1419.   5 rolls.   DP.

Records of International Military Agencies.
RG 333

United Nations Command Korean Armistice Negotiations, 1951–1953.
T1152.   11 rolls.

Records of U.S. Army Commands, 1942–.
RG 338

U.S. Army Investigation and Trial Records of War Criminals

Some records in these publications are from RG 153.
See also RG 238, National Archives Collection of World War II War Crimes Records.

U.S. Army Investigation and Trial Records of War Criminals: *United States of America* v. *Alfons Klein et al.*, Oct. 8–15, 1945 (Case No. 12-449 and 000-12-31).
M1078.   3 rolls.   DP.

U.S. Army Investigation and Trial Records of War Criminals: *United States of America* v. *Kurt Andrae et al.*, Apr. 27, 1945–June 11, 1958 (Case No. 12-481 and 000-50-37).
M1079.   16 rolls.   DP.

U.S. Army Investigation and Trial Records of War Criminals: *United States of America* v. *Franz Auer et al.*, Nov. 1943–July 1958.
M1093.   13 rolls.   DP.

U.S. Army Investigation and Trial Records of War Criminals: *United States of America* v. *Juergen Stroop et al.*, Mar. 29, 1945–Aug. 21, 1957.
M1095.   10 rolls.   DP.

U.S. Army Trials and Post-trial Records of War Criminals: *United States of America* v. *Ernest Dura et al.*, June 9–23, 1947.
M1100.   2 rolls.   DP.

U.S. Army Investigation and Trial Records of War Criminals: *United States of America* v. *Kurt Goebell et al.*, Feb. 6–Mar. 21, 1946, and *United States of America* v. *August Haesiker*, June 26, 1947.
M1103.   7 rolls.   DP.

U.S. Army Investigation and Trial Records of War Criminals: *United States of America* v. *Otto Skorzeny et al.*, July 13, 1945–Dec. 13, 1948.
M1106.   24 cards   DP.
       (microfiche).

Records of the U.S. Army War Crimes Trials: *United States of America* v. *Johann Haider et al.*, Sept. 3–12, 1947.
M1139.   2 rolls.   DP.

Records of the U.S. Army War Crimes Trials: *United States of America* v. *Michael Vogel et al.*, July 8–15, 1947.
M1173.   2 rolls.   DP.

U.S. Army Investigation and Trial Records of War Criminals: *United States of America* v. *Gottfried Weiss et al.*, Nov. 15–Dec. 13, 1945.
M1174.   6 rolls.   DP.

Records of the U.S. Army War Crimes Trials: *United States of America* v. *Hans Joachim Georg Geiger et al.*, July 9–Aug. 5, 1947.
M1191.   2 rolls.

Records of the U.S. Army War Crimes Trials: *United States of America* v. *Friedrick Becker et al.*, July 5, 1945–June 11, 1958.
M1204.   15 rolls.   DP.

Records of the U.S. Army War Crimes Trials: *United States of America* v. *Ernest Angerer et al.*, Nov. 26–Dec. 3, 1946.
M1210.   1 roll.   DP.0.

Reviews of U.S. Army War Crimes Trials in Europe, 1945–1948.
M1217.   5 rolls.   DP.

German Documents Among the War Crimes Records of the Judge Advocate Division, Headquarters, U.S. Army, Europe.
T1021.   20 rolls.

Records of Headquarters U.S. Air Force (Air Staff). RG 341

Project *Bluebook*.
T1206.   94 rolls.

Records of the Bureau of Insular Affairs. RG 350

Index to Official Published Documents Relating to Cuba and the Insular Possessions of the United States, 1876–1906.
M24.   3 rolls.   DP.

Records of the Government of the District of Columbia. RG 351

Records of the City of Georgetown (District of Columbia), 1800–1879.
M605.   49 rolls.   DP.

District of Columbia Building Permits, 1877–1949, and Index, 1877–1958.*
M1116.   283 rolls, 1877–   16mm
       1903 and index;
       681 rolls, July 1,
       1915–Sept. 7, 1949.
*These records continue to be filmed. Contact the Publications Distribution Branch (NECD) for current information on availability.

Records of Interdepartmental and Intradepartmental Committees (State Department). RG 353

State-War-Navy Coordinating Committee (SWNCC) and State-Army-Navy-Air Force Coordinating Committee (SANACC) Decimal Subject Files, 1944–1949.
M1195.   12 rolls.

Minutes of Meetings of the State-War-Navy Coordinating Committee (SWNCC), 1944–1947.
T1194.   1 roll.

Minutes of Meetings of the Subcommittee for the Far East, 1945–1947.
T1198.   1 roll.

Records of the Subcommittee for the Far East, 1945–1948.
T1205.   14 rolls.

Records of the Secretary of State's Staff Committee, 1944–1947.
M1054.   5 rolls.   DP.

Records of the Continental and Confederation Congresses and the Constitutional Convention. RG 360

Papers of the Continental Congress, 1774–1789.
M247.   204 rolls. DP.

Miscellaneous Papers of the Continental Congress, 1774–1789.
M332.   10 rolls.   DP.

Records of the Constitutional Convention of 1787.
M866.   1 roll.   DP.

Treasury Department Collection of Confederate Records. RG 365

Letters Received by the Confederate Secretary of the Treasury, 1861–1865.
M499   57 rolls.   DP.

Letters Sent by the Confederate Secretary of the Treasury, 1861, 1864–1865.
M500.   1 roll.   DP.

Records of the Cotton Bureau of the Trans-Mississippi Department of the Confederate War Department, 1862–1865.
T1129.   50 rolls.

Records of the Defense Nuclear Agency. RG 374
Manhattan Engineer District History.
A1218.   14 rolls.

Records of the U.S. Army Continental Commands, 1821–1920. RG 393
Records of the Tenth Military Department, 1846–1851.
M210.   7 rolls.   DP.

Headquarters Records of Fort Dodge, Kansas, 1866–1882.
M989.   25 rolls. DP.

Letters Sent by the Ninth Military Department, Department of New Mexico, and District of New Mexico, 1849–1890.
M1072.   7 rolls.   DP.

Headquarters Records of Fort Verde, Arizona, 1866–1891.
M1076.   11 rolls. DP.

Headquarters Records of Fort Scott, Kansas, 1869–1873.
M1077.   2 rolls.   DP.

Headquarters Records of Fort Cummings, New Mexico, 1863–1873, 1880–1884.
M1081.   8 rolls.   DP.

Letters Sent, Registers of Letters Received, and Letters Received by Headquarters, Troops in Florida, and Headquarters, Department of Florida, 1850–1858.
M1084.   10 rolls. DP.

Letters Received by Headquarters, District of New Mexico, Sept. 1865–Aug. 1890.
M1088.   65 rolls. DP.

Memoir of Reconnaissances With Maps During the Florida Campaign, Apr. 1854–Feb. 1858.
M1090.   1 roll.   DP.

Letters Sent by the Department of Florida and Successor Commands, Apr. 18, 1861–Jan. 1869.
M1096.   2 rolls.   DP.

Registers of Letters Received by Headquarters, District of New Mexico, Sept. 1865–Aug. 1890.
M1097.   11 rolls. DP.

Register of Letters Received, and Letters Received by Headquarters, Ninth Military Department, 1848–1853.
M1102.   7 rolls.   DP.

Letters Sent by Headquarters, Department of Texas, 1870–1898.
M1114.   10 rolls. DP.

Registers of Letters Received, and Letters Received by Headquarters, Department of New Mexico, 1854–1865.
M1120.   30 rolls. DP.

Letters Sent by the Department of Texas and the Fifth Military District, 1856–1858, 1865–1870.
M1165.   3 rolls.   DP.

Correspondence of the Office of Civil Affairs of the District of Texas, the 5th Military District, and the Department of Texas, 1867–1870.
M1188.   40 rolls. DP.

Headquarters Records of Fort Stockton, Texas, 1867–1886.
M1189.   8 rolls.   DP.

Registers of Letters Received and Letters Received of the Department of Texas, the District of Texas, and the 5th Military District, 1865–1870.
M1193.   33 rolls. DP.

Records of Headquarters, Army of the Southwestern Frontier, and Headquarters, Second and Seventh Military Departments, 1835–1853.
M1302.   8 rolls.   DP.7.

Headquarters Records of the District of the Pecos, 1878–1881.
M1381.   5 rolls.   DP.

Headquarters Records of Fort Gibson, Indian Territory, 1830–1857.
M1466.   6 rolls.   DP.

►Correspondence of the Eastern Division Pertaining to Cherokee Removal, April–December 1838.
M1475.   2 rolls.   DP.

"Special Files" of Headquarters, Division of the Missouri, Relating to Military Operations and Administration, 1863–1885.
M1495.   16 rolls. DP.

Headquarters Records of Fort Sumner, New Mexico, 1862–1869.
M1512.   5 rolls.   DP.

Letters Sent by the Post Commander at Fort Bayard, New Mexico, 1888–1897.
T320.   3 rolls.

Letters Sent, Fort Mojave, Arizona Territory, 1859–1890.
T838.   2 rolls.

Brief Histories of U.S. Army Commands (Army Posts) and Descriptions of Their Records.
T912.   1 roll.

Records of U.S. Army Overseas Operations and Commands, 1898–1942. RG 395
Historical Files of the American Expeditionary Forces in Siberia, 1918–1920.
M917.   11 rolls. DP.

Records of the U.S. Naval Academy. RG 405
Registers of Letters Received and Letters Received by the Superintendent of the U.S. Naval Academy, 1888–1906.
M1018.   89 rolls. DP.

Letters Received by the Superintendent of the U.S. Naval Academy, 1845–1887.
M949.   11 rolls. DP.

Letters Sent by the Superintendent of the U.S. Naval Academy, 1845–1865.
M945.   3 rolls.   DP.

Letters Sent by the Superintendent of the U.S. Naval Academy (Main Series), 1865–1907.
M994.   53 rolls. DP.

U.S. Naval Academy Registers of Delinquencies, 1846–1850, 1853–1882, and Academic and Conduct Records of Cadets, 1881–1908.
M991.   45 rolls. DP.

Records of the Adjutant General's Office, 1917–. RG 407

Cross Index to the Central Files of the Adjutant General's Office, 1917–1939.
T822.   1,956 rolls.

U.S. Army Regulations, Aug. 10, 1920–Dec. 31, 1945.
T978.   15 rolls.

Donated Materials
in the National Archives

➤Naturalization Index of the Superior Court for Los Angeles County, California, 1852–1915.
M1608. 1 roll.

➤Index to Citizens Naturalized in the Superior Court of San Diego, California, 1853–1956.
M1609. 1 roll.

➤Index to Declarations of Intention in the Superior Court of San Diego County, California, 1853–1956.
M1612. 1 roll.

➤Naturalization Records in the Superior Court of San Diego County California, 1883-1958.
M1613. 19 rolls.

➤Naturalization Records of the Superior Court of Los Angeles County, California, 1876–1915.
M1614. 28 rolls.

➤Naturalization Index Cards from the Supreme Court of San Diego County, California, 1929–1956.
M1526. 5 rolls.

Miscellaneous

Microfilm publications in this section are copies of records that belong to no Record Group or are compilations from many Record Groups.

Military Operations of the Civil War: A Guide Index to the Official Records of the Union and Confederate Armies, 1861–1865, Volume I, Conspectus.
M1036. 1 roll. DP.

Official Records of the Union and Confederate Armies, 1861–1865.
M262. 128 rolls. 16mm.

Official Records of the Union and Confederate Navies, 1861–1865.
M275. 31 rolls. 16mm.

Selected Photographs of Calvin Coolidge, 1917–1943.
M867. 1 roll. DP.

Selected Photographs of Franklin D. Roosevelt, 1913–1945.
M865. 1 roll. DP.

Selected Photographs of Harry S. Truman, 1885–1953.
M835. 2 rolls. DP.

Selected Photographs of Dwight D. Eisenhower, 1943–1961.
M868. 1 roll. DP.

The Territorial Papers of the United States.
M721. 16 rolls. DP.

The Territorial Papers of the United States: Iowa, 1838–1846.
M325. 102 rolls. DP.

The Territorial Papers of the United States: Minnesota, 1849–1858.
M1050. 11 rolls.

The Territorial Papers of the United States: Oregon, 1848–1859.
M1049. 12 rolls.

A Microfilm Supplement to the Territorial Papers of the United States: Wisconsin, 1836–1848.
M236. 122 rolls. DP.

Examples of Records in the National Archives Frequently Used in Genealogical Research.
T325. 1 roll.

Compilation of Tennessee Census Reports, 1820.
T911. 1 roll.

➤Wisconsin Territorial Censuses of 1836, 1838, 1842, 1846, and 1847.
M1809. 3 rolls.

National Archives Teaching Aids: Selected State Department Records.
T987. 6 rolls.

Historical Sketches for Jurisdictional and Subject Headings Used for the Letters Received by the Office of Indian Affairs, 1824–1880.
T1105. 1 roll.

The Papers of Henry William Ellsworth, 1845–1849.
A1176. 4 rolls.

Subject-Author-Title Catalog of Selected Publications of the Federal Government, ca. 1900–ca. 1950.
T1203. 64 rolls.

Papers Relating to the Administration of the U.S. Patent Office During the Superintendency of William Thornton, 1802–1828: A Guide to Accompany Federal Documentary Microfilm Edition No. 1. 5 rolls. DP.

General Correspondence of the Alaskan Territorial Governor, 1909–1958.
M939. 378 rolls. DP.

Records of the Alaskan Territorial Legislature, 1913–1953.
M1012. 21 rolls. DP.

Chronological Files of the Alaskan Governor, 1884–1919.
T1200. 44 rolls.

Correspondence of the Secretary of Alaska, 1900–1913.
T1201. 20 rolls.

Belgian Foreign Ministry.
Records Relating to North America, 1834–1899, From the Archives of the Belgian Ministry of Foreign Affairs.
T125. 9 rolls.

Papers of R. Dorsey Mohun, 1892–1913.
T294. 3 rolls.

Republic of the Philippines.
Philippine Insurgent Records, 1896–1901, With Associated Records of the U.S. War Department, 1900–1906.
M254. 643 rolls. DP.

Records From More Than One Record Group.

RG 38, 80, and 313

Records Relating to U.S. Navy Fleet Problems I to XXII, 1923–1941.
M964. 36 rolls. DP.

RG 39 and 53

Central Treasury Records of the Continental and Confederation Governments Relating to Foreign Affairs, 1775–1787.
M1004. 3 rolls. DP.

RG 39, 53, and 217

Central Treasury Records of the
Continental and Confederation
Governments, 1775–1789.
M1014.   23 rolls.   DP.

Central Treasury Records of the
Continental and Confederation
Governments Relating to Military
Affairs, 1775–1789.
M1015.   7 rolls.   DP.

RG 45 and 80

Navy Department General Orders,
1863–1948.
M984.   3 rolls.   DP.

RG 45, 71, and 80

Navy Department General Orders and
Circulars, 1798–1862.
M977.   2 rolls.   DP.

RG 48 and 75

Reports of Inspections of the Field
Jurisdictions of the Office of Indian
Affairs, 1873–1900.
M1070.   60 rolls.   DP.

RG 92, 93, and 94

Letters, Orders for Pay, Accounts,
Receipts, and Other Supply Records
Concerning Weapons and Military
Stores, 1776–1801.
M927.   1 roll.   DP.

RG 94 and 393

Descriptive Commentaries From the
Medical Histories of Posts.
M903.   5 rolls.   DP.

RG 94 and 391

Returns From Regular Army Cavalry
Regiments, 1833–1916.
M744.   117 rolls.   DP.

RG 24, 25, 94, 107, 153, 391, and 393

Documents Relating to the Military
and Naval Service of Blacks Awarded
the Congressional Medal of Honor
From the Civil War to the Spanish
American War.
M929.   4 rolls.   DP.

Annual Reports of the War
Department, 1822–1907.
M997.   164 rolls.   DP.

RG 94 and 149

Selected Documents Relating to
Blacks Nominated for Appointment to
the U.S. Military Academy During the
19th Century, 1870–1887.
M1002.   21 rolls.   DP.

RG 24 and 94

Records Relating to Military Service in
the Civil War of Medal of Honor
Winners From Michigan.
T732.   5 rolls.

RG 156 and 159

Summary Statements of Quarterly
Returns of Ordnance and Ordnance
Stores on Hand in Regular and
Volunteer Army Organizations,
1862–1867, 1870–1876.
M1281.   8 rolls.   DP.

Alphabetical List of Record Groups Contained in This Catalog

Numerical List of Microfilm Publication Numbers

Index

MICROFILM ORDER

(Prices subject to change)

Microfilm publication numbers (preceded by an "M" or "T" are assigned to each microfilm publication. Please enter the microfilm publication number(s) and roll number(s) in the proper columns. Because we accept orders for individual rolls, as well as for complete microfilm publications, we must know which rolls you wish to purchase.

Effective May 15, 1996, the price for each roll of microfilm is $34 for U.S. orders. The price is $39 per roll for foreign orders. Shipping is included. These prices are subject to change without notice. For current price information, write to National Archives Publications Distribution (NECD), Room G9, Seventh and Pennsylvania Avenue, NW, Washington, DC 20048, or call 1-800-234-8861 (in the Washington, DC, metropolitan area, 202-501-7190).

Sample of correctly completed form.

MICRO. PUB. NUMBER	ROLL NUMBER(S)	PRICE
T624	1138	$34
T1270	88 – 89	$68

Additional order forms are available upon request.

ORDERED BY *(Include organization if shipping to a business address.)*

Name	
Organization *(if applicable)*	
Address *(Number and Street)*	
City, State, & ZIP Code	
Daytime Telephone Number *(Include Area Code)*	

PAYMENT TYPE

Send your order to:

CREDIT CARD

Check one and enter card number below. ☐ VISA ☐ MasterCard

Exp. Date

Signature

National Archives Trust Fund Cashier (NAJC) Washington, D.C. 20408 (Credit card orders may be faxed to 202-501-7170)

OTHER

☐ Check ☐ Money Order
Make payable to: National Archives Trust Fund.

Amount Enclosed $

National Archives Trust Fund P.O. Box 100793 Atlanta, GA 30384-0793

IDENTIFY THE ROLLS YOU WISH TO ORDER

MICRO. PUB. NUMBER	ROLL NUMBER(S)	PRICE	MICRO. PUB. NUMBER	ROLL NUMBER(S)	PRICE
				Subtotal *(this column)*	
				Subtotal from first column	
	Subtotal *(this column)*			**TOTAL PRICE**	

NATIONAL ARCHIVES TRUST FUND BOARD   NATF Form 326 (rev. 5/96)